AF483705

IMAGINATION OF A SMALL CHILD

AND

FAIRY TALE AND A CHILD

INSTITUTE FOR CONTEMPORARY PEDAGOGY
HIGHER PEDAGOGICAL SCHOOL, BELGRADE

EDITORS: MILORAD VANLIĆ AND DR. SLOBODAN POPOVIĆ

PUBLISHED IN SERBIAN IN 1937
RAJKOVIĆ PUBLISHING BOOKSTORE, 16 TERAZIJE, BELGRADE, SERBIA

RUŽA LERINC

IMAGINATION OF A SMALL CHILD

A CONTRIBUTION TO CHILD PSYCHOLOGY AND PEDAGOGY

AND

FAIRY TALE AND A CHILD

PUBLISHED SEPARATELY IN TEACHER – 1940 EDITION

TRANSLATED AND EDITED
BY MIRNA HIRSCHL KRIŽNIĆ

DANCING LEAVES PRESS
2026

ISBN Number: 979-8-9929264-4-6

Book design by Robert Perry
Robert Perry Book Design
Palo Alto, California
robertperrybookdesign.com

SELECTION OF PUBLICATIONS: FULL CITATION

***Imagination of a Small Child: A Contribution
to Child Psychology and Pedagogy***
by Ruža Lerinc

Published in Serbian in 1937
by Rajković Publishing Bookstore
16 Terazije, Belgrade, Serbia
through the Institute for Cotemporary Pedagogy
Higher Pedagogical School, Belgrade
Editors: Milorad Vanlić and Dr. Slobodan Popović.

"Fairy Tale and a Child"
by Ruža Lerinc

Published separately in 1940,
in *Teacher,* 9-10, pp. 529-533.

Translated and edited in this book by Mirna Hirschl Križnić.

To Ruža, who embodied
the best of the human spirit

FOREWORD

Ruža Lerinc is my maternal aunt. I remember, as a child, the pages torn from her book. Loose, out of order, and yellowed, they survived World War II, numerous moves, and even a flood—obstinate and incomplete, as only relics can be. Five years ago, I discovered her out-of-print book on the internet. Perhaps someone had cleaned out their attic. The book—its cover in the Art Deco style befitting the era—was available for purchase, in Serbian, printed in the Cyrillic alphabet.

I knew then that someday I would translate it into English, leaving it as a precious inheritance for my children and grandchildren.

Imagination of a Small Child (*Mašta Maloga Deteta*), the best-known and most influential work by Ruža Lerinc, was published in Belgrade, in 1937. Conceived primarily as a scientific study of the psychology of small children, this book is based on her own detailed personal experiences and observations of real cases as well as on the results of testing. Her study also draws on the most advanced theories of the prominent child psychologists of the time, interpreting them and measuring them against her own findings. Since she was fluent in German and French, she was able to introduce her readers to new developments in the field of child psychology through books not yet translated. Thus, her students, whom she was preparing to become teachers themselves, could use her book as a textbook replete with cutting-edge information in contemporary child psychology.

To quote Prof. Dr. Nada Todorov (see Notes):

> "Lerinc's book deserves attention for the innovations it offers in the scientific sense, particularly regarding the early development of reception theory … The research published in her scholarly work "Fairy Tale and a Child" is pioneering because Lerinc raises the question of the literary work as a communicator, with a child, rather than the adult, being placed at the

center of the education process, thus anticipating Jauss' theory of reception—a backbone of contemporary education—some forty years ahead of its time."

After persistent research, I uncovered the text of the "Fairy Tale and a Child" included in this translation.

As for the rest of her scientific writings and literary works—short stories, fairy tales, and poems (many written for children), plays, essays, political discourses, and translations—there were at least twenty-five. Many early works were published under pseudonyms, mostly "R. L." I was able to retrieve only their titles, as cited in other publications. In this search, I was aided by a steady stream of articles and commemorative works reflecting on her heroic life and achievements, some written by her colleagues and former students, others by scholars in the fields of literature, education, and psychology.

Ruža Lerinc was born on July 21, 1896, in Nadudvar, a small town in eastern Hungary. She grew up in Slavonski Brod, Croatia, where she attended elementary and middle school. From 1913 to 1917, she studied in Zagreb at the Women's Lyceum with a pedagogical orientation, which later enabled her to work as a teacher. It so happened that the Lyceum moved in 1913 into a new building in the Old Town of Zagreb—the very building that, 35 years later, housed the high school I attended. I didn't know it then, but it moves me now to think that our paths, separated by time, crossed within the same walls.

The 1920s, for Ruža, were a period of gathering teaching experience at different locations, pursuing graduate studies, and writing for local magazines. Her duties ranged from teaching psychology, pedagogy, methodology of schoolwork, German, and Latin to serving as a school director and head librarian. In her spare time, she continued her studies, was active in the local Jewish community, and contributed articles to local journals. After graduating in 1930 from the Higher Pedagogical School in Belgrade, she was appointed professor at the State Teachers' School in Aleksinac, where she remained for the rest of her career.

Ever socially conscious, Ruža was actively involved in groups opposing smoking and alcoholism, at a time when such causes were not popular. She also conducted literacy classes and advocated for the advancement of women's position in society. Seeking ways to improve the lives of both women and children, she founded the first nursery school in Aleksinac.

The nursery school was a model of modern education—a success in more than one sense. It had an impact on the socioeconomic base of the families involved: It provided an early start in schooling for many children while freeing their mothers to pursue further education, and in many cases, to become educators themselves. As a byproduct, it offered a broad sampling base conducive to the author's scholarly endeavors, as well as a source of fieldwork for future teachers.

This was also the time of her deepening involvement in youth groups advocating social justice and political awareness, especially concerning the dangers of fascism. As the thirties wore on and the invasion of Poland took place, she became an essential member of a group called "Progress," whose membership included both teachers and students. The group evolved from a theoretical platform into an antifascist resistance movement.

In April 1941, the Germans occupied Aleksinac, bringing persecution and the smell of death.

In June 1941, after almost ten years at her post, she—being Jewish—was dismissed from her position. It didn't take the authorities long to place her on the wanted list. Destitute and ill, she took refuge in a small town near Aleksinac with a former student, Milica Cvetanović. At the same time, the students from the inner circle of "Progress"—political activists and resistance leaders— were in danger of being expelled from school, persecuted, and interrogated.

In the words of Dragomir Filipović (see Notes), a "Progress" member and eyewitness:

> "Gone were peaceful, beautiful school days, filled with learning, passionate reading of literature, and political discussions. There was no peace and tranquility for others either, especially those from whom we received instructions.... The interrogations were daily and systematic, full of pitfalls. Professor Ruža Lerinc was constantly with us during those days, cheering us on. I remember what she said: 'None of this is your fault. They cannot exclude you from school because you were friends with books, because you wanted to know more.... She seems to have naively believed it herself; otherwise, she would not have allowed the police chief to easily get hold of her and hand her over to the Germans so early in the occupation.... Everything ended with us being expelled from school, with our vilification in front of the students of the class we belonged to. All the professors of the school, with the exception of Ruža Lerinc, complied with this verdict—in fact, the entire teaching council. The director even managed to keep his position, then and later ... I sensed then, thanks to the selfless behavior of Prof. Lerinc, the greatness and power of a true educational calling."

Hoping to encourage and aid her students, and believing that the attack on communists and Jews had passed and that she would no longer be pursued, she returned to Aleksinac and was promptly apprehended on or about August 8th. What followed were two weeks of imprisonment, about which I do not have any information, except that during that time, members of the resistance assassinated the county governor who collaborated with the occupying forces. The German punitive expedition arrived two days later and arrested all Jewish families in Aleksinac, along with a hundred prominent non-Jewish citizens. Then they broke into the prison.

Ruža Lerinc was shot during the night of August 23 and hanged on the flagpole in front of the school where she had taught for almost ten years—a brutal warning to other resistance fighters. She was only forty-five years old.

Her memory is still venerated. Hardly a decade goes by without some major tribute to her professional achievements and to her as a person. To mention only a few:

A review of her work (see Notes) by a fellow writer in the field of child psychology, Prof. Dr. Nada Todorov;

A commemorative article (see Notes) dedicated to Ruža Lerinc on the occasion of 120 years of the Teacher's School in Aleksinac;

A chapter (see Notes) devoted to her in the comprehensive history of the Aleksinac area including her biography, professional achievements, and the quotes from her contemporaries;

In 1959, a memorial plaque was created honoring educators from Niš and the surrounding area (including Aleksinac), who were killed as resistance fighters. My mother and grandmother were present at the unveiling ceremony.

In 2022, a video documentary (see Notes) was compiled by the history professors and enacted by the students at the still active State Teachers' school in Aleksinac.

Every time I think of Ruža, I am humbled. Despite her tragic story, just remembering that such people exist fills me with hope that goodness still lives in human beings. There is reason to get up in the morning and open the window to a new day. Her spirit endures.

—Mirna Hirschl Križnić

CONTENTS

IMAGINATION OF A SMALL CHILD

INTRODUCTION

Perhaps in nothing does a small child differ more from an adult than in the role that imagination plays in his life (see Notes). Adults use imagination to bring artistic creations to life, to understand them, and to apply it in scientific and practical pursuits. It propels them forward, enriching their lives along the way.

For the child, however, imagination permeates every aspect of life. It plays a key role in helping him engage with and understand the world. It shapes the early years through its vivid activity, expands his narrow horizons, and offers profound spiritual riches. We might say that imagination is the wizard that transforms childhood—when viewed from the distance of adulthood—into a lost paradise, unless it was truly unbearable due to misery and hardship.

This general description of the importance of imagination in childhood calls for a closer examination of how a child's imagination differs from the phantasy life of an adult. This work will focus solely on aspects relevant to the workings of imagination in children up to the age of seven, as it is precisely during this phase of life that the qualities described above are most evident.

Moreover, the seventh year marks a decisive point in a child's development. With the beginning of formal schooling, the children come into much closer contact with the realities of life. By this time, they are sufficiently developed to approach the world with greater capacity and comprehension.

In order to better understand the characteristics of imagination in children, we will briefly examine how the same functions in adults.

Imagination is a combinative ability that draws its material from the representational life of the mind. It disassembles and reassembles what it finds in that spirit into creations that, by their combination, bear the mark of a different whole than the parts themselves, presenting something new.

In adults, the creative work of imagination is usually guided by a goal and influenced by the will. The will affects the creation by controlling the act of combination, while memory provides material and aids the process by allowing past experiences to serve as a guide in developing new ideas. This mirrors the same basic ability of the human spirit to engage in combinatory thinking, although the constructs used by thinking and imagining differ.

The emotions also play a large role in this process and not only because they provide the necessary impetus for the creating process, but also because they deeply influence the act of creation itself. It is well known that many works of art originate from this emotional wellspring. The individual who creates is personally connected to his work; success brings joy, while failure brings pain and anguish. There is a strong emotional bond between creators and their creations.

Even beyond purposeful, goal-oriented creativity, whether in the arts or other areas of life, imagination plays an important role in an individual's life. It is involved in what is known as the "building castles in the air," when a young person envisions his future life, forges various plans, struggles for independence, and in many other aspects of life. Therefore, the role of imagination in human lives is immense.

THE FEATURES OF CHILDREN'S IMAGINATION

Illusion and Illusionism

No matter how lively an adult's imagination may be, as long as they are mentally sane, they will almost always differentiate their imaginative creations from real observations and experiences. This is because they possess an inherent sense of differentiation between the real and the unreal, the actual and the invented. Do human beings naturally carry this sense within them from birth or is it something they learn over time? It seems that a child must acquire this distinction along with many other things. I am saying "it seems" because this cannot be reliably determined. For the time being, it remains only a theory whose plausibility is supported by frequent observations of children's lives. Perhaps the following example provided by German psychologist Karl Bühler, relevant to our discourse, can reinforce this understanding:

"I observed an unusual phenomenon in a two-year-old girl. She had just returned from a walk and was running around exuberantly, when she suddenly stopped in the middle of the room, as if frozen in place. She bent both arms at the elbows and held them slightly away from her body, like the wings of a young bird. She was visibly excited—her eyes widened and focused, and in a trembling voice she shouted 'So la la' which in baby language meant 'soldiers are singing.' She repeated these three words five or six times until I finally managed to calm her down. At that moment, no soldiers' singing could be heard, nor was there anything in the present situation that could have reminded her of soldiers or singing.

It was established later that, about 45 minutes earlier while walking with her nanny, she had encountered soldiers who were singing—an event that, although it was not rare, would always make her very happy. Nothing else special happened. But what could this particular encounter have meant to the child? Her nervous excitement was so great, that we, for our part, tried to avoid any occasion for further recollection. Yet, she repeated the same overly exuberant scene that evening, the next day, and the day after, when it happened to be raining, so that she could not have seen or heard any soldiers. The episode occurred a few more times, her excitement gradually decreasing."

This much is certain: what happened here was an extremely vivid internal recovery of the former experience. Similarly, we adults sometimes find ourselves unable to shake off an important or even a trivial thought, such as a melody that lingers in the mind, as annoying as a fly.

This event imposed itself inwardly on the child again and again. Science calls this phenomenon **perseverance**. What is unusual here is only the excitement for which there was no external reason. The child had experienced a similar kind of recollection a long time ago. According to the theory of

Bühler[1], the child may have realized for the first time that this vividly recurring inner event stood in opposition to her perception of the present situation which it contradicted, and this realization was the cause of her excitement. If our explanation is accurate, then, to quote Bühler, "We can see in such events the moment of birth and the labor pains of consciously distinguishing representation from perception."

The sense of astonishment in this very young child proves that the entire experience meant to her something big and new. For the first time, she became aware of a "touching point" between two different worlds—the world of reality and the world of appearance. Her small being was suddenly imbued with the realization of the difference between them.

William Stern[2] more decisively advocates the idea that gaining insight into the **objective** and the **subjective** is necessary through life experience and it must be cultivated and strengthened to develop a consciousness that remains vigilant in determining the nature of any given experience—whether it belongs to the province of certainty or a province of mere appearance. How often does it happen to us adults that we deal with illusions that, in the end, do not hold up, only because we maintain a critical objectivity.

To offer a personal example: below the text of an article in *Politics,* I saw a photo with a caption "Wounded during the fight on the street." The article next to it discussed the situation in Germany. At first, I assumed the picture depicted a scene from Germany. I would have continued to believe it, had I not sensed an inconsistency between the article's content and my interpretation of the image, which prompted me to take a closer look.

I cite this example only to illustrate that critical awareness is not always equally vigilant at every moment. A child who lives almost exclusively in the present—unconcerned with the past and unaware of the value of the future—has no capacity to verify certain contents of consciousness. William Stern, (ibid.) expounds: "To these little, as yet undeveloped human beings, everything intensely experienced is real, and it remains real as long as the child immerses himself in these experiences." A child can completely "give" himself over to the interpretation of his imagination; for the time being, it is his reality—no less objective then the food on his plate, an event recalled from memory, or a blow which causes him pain.

At first, a child's understanding of any event naturally includes a need to have confidence and to believe in himself. The strength of this belief depends less on objective facts and more on the subjective intensity of the child's awareness. The separation of these two worlds begins quite early. Often, a small child

---

1 Karl Bühler: *Abriss Geistigen Entwicklung des Kindes* (see Notes),1927, p. 83.

2 William Stern: *Psychologie der frühen Kindheit*, 1930.

encounters obstacles and difficulties that must be overcome, and gradually, a partition begins to form between the objective and the subjective. Nothing happens all at once. One could say that the whole pre-school age is marked by this "touching" of the objective and the subjective—this wavering between the extremes.

At one moment, the child embraces the creations of his imagination as reality, fully living in them; in the next, he recognizes that they are made up and do not correspond to reality.

In the first case, the child is immersed in his creation, believing wholeheartedly in its reality. In the second, he rises above it and takes control of it. The first case is an **illusion**. To quote Karl Groos: "Illusion, in the true sense, consists of being deceived about reality—that is, one simply perceives what is given as something else, something it is not, and thus reacts to the wrong perception exactly as if it were the correct one."[1]

In the second case, there is an awareness of the true meaning of things, but it remains more in the background, while the prevailing meaning is being the assigned one—whether it arises from external circumstances or internal reasons. This transitional state is also known to adults. It manifests itself, for example, when we momentarily perceive something familiar as something else. Thus, a dress draped over a chair may at first evoke the image of a man sitting on a chair. Of course, such self-deception is not intentional. We soon recognize the reality of the situation, but we can intentionally repeat this deception of seeing one thing represented in another, such as is the case with the dress.

A child delights in this kind of self-deception. According to the German esthetician Konrad Land, a fellow psychologist Karl Groos calls this phenomenon **"conscious self-deception."** The child loves it because it empowers him, helps him overcome reality, and expands his narrow, limited life. The degrees of fluctuation between reality, illusion and self-deception are demonstrated in the following example:

Mile (3 years, 9 months) is walking with his father and me. He wants his father to buy him both a teddy bear and a bunny so that the two toys can have each other for company. His father asks him, if he loves his teddy so much, why did he poke out his eyes and otherwise damage the teddy he already has. I asked in surprise, "Weren't you sorry to torture the teddy?" To this he quickly replies, as if instructing me, that the teddy was already dead. Here we see how the child's perception of reality shifts from moment to moment, almost without transition.

---

1 Karl Groos: *Das Seelenleben des Kindes*, 1921.

In another case, an almost-five-year-old girl insists that we cover her teddy bear, which is lying on the couch in a cold room. When asked why, she replies with conviction, "He feels things too."

An aunt was telling the *Puss in Boots* fairy tale to her niece (6 years old) and her nephew (7 years old). The children adore their aunt and their visiting grandmother, and they wish both of them could come more often. But the grandmother is frail and sickly, making such visits too difficult for her. Before departing, the girl expresses her great desire to have such boots that make anything possible, and not only that, but she also says that on the way home, she will keep an eye out for the boots that Puss may have lost. Her brother latches on to this idea, and together, they excitedly revel in their imagined marvelous luck in advance, weaving the tall tale even further. After all, children's belief in Santa Claus, who rewards the good and punishes the naughty, as well as the tale of the stork and other are fables based on similar assumptions.

The children mentioned in this work are of various ages, and this is intentional. The order of presentation illustrates that the phenomena described here emerge early and span the entirety of early childhood. The two following examples further demonstrate how a small child uses illusion:

A two-year-old boy sits across from me, tears the paper into shreds and, smiling, hands them to me to eat, saying in his childish language that it is good. But when I take those same pieces of paper and bring them to his mouth, he pulls away, protesting and shouting, "Kaka be, kaka be," meaning "it's not good, it's dirty." There was clearly an intention to play here, as it would be difficult to think he was trying to deceive me. That would require attributing too much sophistication to a two-year-old child. He was playing—assigning a meaning to the paper that it doesn't actually have, only to reveal it was just a play by refusing to treat it as food. This example illustrates that even a small child has some awareness of the difference between objective and subjective, between perception and imagination.

A three-and-a-half year old girl teaches me how to play:

"You sleep. That's your crib."
She points to a spot on the table. "Go to sleep."
She then opens an eyeglass case, which makes a small banging
 sound.
"Now make believe you are scared. Shoot the thieves." The phrase
"make believe" shows that the child is consciously engaging in
illusion. Yet, just the night before, this same child was deeply offended
and nearly cried when I didn't pay enough attention to Betsy—her toy
savings bank—which was already broken in one spot.
She declared:
"Betsy is staring at you. She is upset because you don't love her."

8

The awareness of illusion is even more evident in the following example as the child herself exposes it.

> The children have gathered around Ljerka (3 years, 1 month). She wants to play a dwarf who scares her little cousin, so she makes terrible grimaces. The older children pretend to be frightened and scream, prompting her to shout:
> "It's me, Ljerka. Don't be afraid, I'm just kidding."

These examples show that even older children can present details from an imagined world as if they were real. Yet from an early age, depending on their desires or circumstances, children are aware of the difference between these two worlds. They move fluidly between these extremes. It is not a problem for a child that his teddy bear is both alive and dead at the same time. Depending on the intensity of his emotions, desires, or the situation, either believing his illusion or the recognition of reality will prevail. A small child always chooses according to his own interests, placing himself at the center.

We know that there are adults—whose intelligence we cannot deny—in whom a single unexpected thought, perhaps connected with a face they like, can provoke a storm of feelings, a strange agitation that weakens their reasoning. How else can we explain an outpouring of unjustified jealousy if not by the dominance of self-illusion, which, in the moment of emotional arousal, suppresses critical thinking. Some may argue that this comparison is too bold, as it compares unrelated states. And yet, an analogy can be drawn.

A child's **illusionism** arises from inexperience, the nature of emotions, and the vividness of imagination. In an adult, when this condition occurs—whether for a longer or shorter duration—strong emotion distorts reality and suppresses reasonable thought. In adult, critical consciousness momentarily retreats before the onslaught of feelings; in children, it is still weak because it is in the process of developing. Fully immersed in the world of play, a small child surrenders to it entirely, unaware of such extremes.

"Sometimes a child, locked in its own self, believes his own fiction and plays with it. At other times, when he comes into contact with the thoughts of others, he forgets and adopts another point of view" states Jean Piaget.[1]

This feature of imagination—to create fictions—enables the child to see things as what they are not and to perceive details that aren't actually there. We can thank this illusionism for much of the cuteness with which children bring joy to the adults around them. This capacity for illusion enriches a child's otherwise limited life in every way. The weak child, who depends on the help of adults in everything, thus becomes strong—nursing and caring for dolls, traveling, managing work, and more. He becomes a father, mother, postman, chauffeur,

---

1 Jean Piaget: *Le jugement et le raisonnement chez l'enfant*, 1924.

or assumes any other role, almost as if summoning things and people to do his bidding. Thus, the child owes many of his joys and pleasures to this remarkable feature of imagination.

Both older and younger children find great pleasure in **looking at pictures**. In the psychology of childhood, images have been used as a tool for studying various aspects of mental life. I chose the observation of pictures as a means of examining children's imagination, because it is self-evident that this particular activity will most clearly reveal the characteristic aspects of their inner world.

The idea is not new. William Stern, in his *Psychologie der Frühen Kindheit*, devotes an entire chapter to it. He arrives at some interesting conclusions, many of which are confirmed by his study. Naturally, a child's entire mind is engaged in this kind of activity, making picture observation a frequently used method for exploring other aspects of a child's psyche. Imagination plays a key role in bringing the scenes in the pictures to life and in grasping their deeper meaning.

For this purpose, the children I worked with were first shown the illustrations from the well known fairy tales *The Wolf and the Seven Little Kids* and *Puss in Boots*, followed by images from a newly told fairy tale, and finally, pages from the children's picture book *The Story of the Root Children* by Sibille von Olfers.[1] I need to say a bit more here about *The Story of the Root Children*. The illustrations in it symbolically depict nature in all four seasons as seen through the eyes of a small child. For example, the arrival of spring is depicted as a procession of children and insects. Leading the procession are children dressed in green followed by bugs, and then a row of girls wearing dresses that match the colors of the flowers they each symbolically carry in their hands.

I showed these pictures to the children without any previous interpretation because I wanted to give their imagination free rein.

I mostly questioned the children from the nursery school in our town (Aleksinac, Serbia). It was not difficult to make friends with these little creatures. My presence and the activities we shared were a welcome change for them, and we quickly became good friends. As a result, the work took on a spontaneous, almost unintentional quality. I was also interested in children even younger than those in the nursery school, so I'll begin this presentation with the youngest child I interviewed.

Ljerka (2 years, 11 months), for example, observes a picture of children approaching their mothers to show off their dresses. There is a woman with a basket in front of her, full of knitting. In the upper part of the picture, a path is visible. Ljerka spontaneously comments while looking at the path in the picture:

---

1 Sibille von Olfers: *Etwas von den Wurzelkindern*, 1908.

"Lots of children. Because we were in Big Moravica when we were big and swimming. They put on the little hooded coat and sit down. Sit down, had a good time. The basket had little pastries and wine." (She recalls Little Red Riding Hood. She looks at each picture for a short time. At first, she notices multiple details in one picture, but later she perceives fewer, probably due to fatigue.)

She perceives actions and explains them. She speaks impulsively, but her observations often serve to merely revive memories—recalling a familiar fairy tale or a recent event. Her descriptions are egocentric; the picture functions more as a trigger for her imagination, allowing her to weave many of her own thoughts into what she sees. In the process, the actual details of the image are often overlooked. Her observation is accompanied by laughter, movement, and joyful exclamations. At times, it even seemed as though she believed the faces in the pictures were alive. At one point, she asked "What is the dear grandma saying?"

Mara (3 years, 6 months) looks at the picture titled "A Girl Cooking Lunch" from *Politics for Children*. The first time, she describes the actions in the picture almost accurately, except that she replaces the girl with a doll and adds a pillow that isn't actually there. Her second interpretation is much more subjective. This time, pointing to the figures on the picture, Mara says: "She" (the doll) "is asking whether Daddy is home." The mother (the girl in the picture) answers, "He'll arrive soon."

The first description is a consequence of an inaccurate observation, while the second is an illusion, as she brings her own life experiences into the scene—such as asking her mother when Daddy is coming home.

The above examples reflect the **illusionism** of a young child's imagination: **infusing perception with subjectivity**, animating scenes, describing actions with varying interpretations of the same elements, and simultaneously blending these into the act of observation. All of this may give the impression of a rich imagination, but in fact, it primarily reveals its remarkable flexibility.

All preschool-aged children share the challenge of incomplete perception. Much of what seems fantastical in their descriptions often comes down to the fact that they either do not have a clear mental picture of the object or do not observe it carefully. Instead, they intend to interpret what they see almost instantly, in whatever way first comes to mind. However, there are significant differences in how this manifests.

Some deviations are minor—one can at least detect a resemblance between the child's mental representation and an actual appearance of the object. Others, however, are, one might even say, incredible. Let us compare these two cases, for example:

A boy (5 years old) interprets a picture, by saying:
"Girls are gone to bed," then elaborates, "a woman, a lamp. They (the girls) washed themselves, lit a candle, then lay down to sleep."
A second boy (7 years old) simply lists objects without describing any actions:
"Woman,
house (for a bug),
mouse (for a child).
The child (sleeping).
Dog (for a child)."
In the first case, we can see how the child likely draws on his own experiences—washing before bed, for instance—and how he sometimes fails to fully perceive the image's details. In contrast, the substitutions made by the second boy, who is two years older, indicate incomplete observation. At the same time, they suggest the possibility of a developmental delay. (This assumption, based solely on picture interpretation, seems accurate, as it is supported by the teacher's independent assessment of the child.)

The children examined in the nursery school were between five and seven years old, with the exception of one four-year-old. The materials used in the observations were primarily drawn from the book *The Story of the Root Children*. Analysis of the illustrated fairy tales confirmed several findings:

Children's engagement with the pictures can be further categorized as follows: The incorporation of subjective elements—such as those seen in the two girls previously mentioned—continues, but gradually diminishes over time. Even among children who are careful observers, what they see may still evoke personal experiences. However, they now consciously place these memories alongside what they actually perceive in the image, rather than merging them instinctively.

A girl (6 years, 4 months) looks at a picture depicting the awakening of nature and says: "Daddy takes us for a walk too," but she makes this comment only after describing the action in the picture, unlike the younger child aged 2 years and 11 months, who, upon seeing the path in the image, does not mention it at all, but instead immediately recalls his own experience saying, "We were in Velika Moravica."

At this stage, clearer differences emerge in how children observe the pictures. Some bring the scenes more vividly to life, others remain more reserved. One young viewer may be content to simply describe the action and explain what happens and why—inasmuch as he understands it. Another, more absorbed by the scene, adds details, gestures, and even introduces direct speech; one could say that he is living the scene in the picture.

In one illustration, a ladybug lands on a boy's back. Velibor (6 years, 6 months) notices it and adds that the little boy is shouting, "Fly away, fly away ladybug." In the second picture, a snail can be seen with its head turned to the child. While describing the scene, Velibor mimics the same gesture and says, "He will not sting," then goes on to explain to me that a snail does not bite. Thus, keen, accurate perception is closely linked with the animation of the scene and the child's personal engagement with the details of the depicted actions.

At the end of the book, when the children return to their mother, he adds: "Good children, brought a butterfly, then thanked their mother," even though the children have nothing in their hands. He introduces elements into his description that might belong in a fairy tale. Or in heavens. The children are little angels, the Mother reminds one of the Mother of God, and so on.

Here's how the other boy (also 6 years, 6 months old) speaks: He describes actions and, at times, explains why things happen a certain way:
"Grandmother sat down. She is putting on her glasses.
The children are lining up to show her how beautiful their dresses are."
He sees things as they are. At the same time, he also knows how to immerse himself in a story. While looking at the illustrations from *The Wolf and the Seven Little Goats*, he remarked:
"The Wolf says: 'Now I'm going to eat you.' The Baker replies:
'Why should you eat me? Here's your bread—eat that instead.'"
Here, the imagination is calm and remains within the bounds of reality, though it still reflects the characteristic imagination of a child that age.

This is how Zagorka (7 years old) describes the same picture:
"Here is the child's mother. She is crocheting. This bug is rolling the yarn, and another one is just standing in front of the basket. These girls are showing their mother the dresses they sewed."
Then, pointing to the candles, she says:
"It was probably a holiday."
Her perception is generally quite accurate, though at times, she succumbs to illusion. It is evident from her entire description that she grasps the connection between the images (though not their symbolism) and that, by stating "it was probably a holiday," she is not making a definitive claim children often make when explaining an action, but rather expressing a thoughtful possibility.

Another 7-year-old girl also describes the scenes in the picture, but she never explains why things happen. She focuses on what she sees. Her younger brother, aged six, similarly describes actions without adding subjective details, unlike the children mentioned earlier. In citing these examples, I have chosen the ones that seemed most representative, as they highlight what appears to be most typical.

Despite the incompleteness of children's observation typical at this age, their imagination is remarkably lively and easily transferable. Their subjectivity is expressed through the incorporation of personal memories.

They supplement reality, add what they know about objects, and enliven scenes with their own experiences. When explaining things, children rarely offer suppositions—instead, they confidently assert whatever seems true to them. For example, one girl explained that a tree was bare in spring because the caterpillars had devastated it.

However, the developmental trajectory moves increasingly toward reality. More and more often, a child becomes aware of things as they are—though not entirely. The tendency to embellish reality with fantasy persists to some degree even into later schooling. This is the general course of how the recognition of reality develops. At the same time, the collected material shows that the individual character of imagination emerges early on. All sufficiently developed children, in terms of perception, reach the level of action—they observe and explain what they see. The key difference lies in how they interpret what they perceive.

The children who bring a great deal of personal expression to their observations and are deeply affected by the images, are a small minority. (In our study of this age group, only Velibor—and to a lesser extent one other child—exhibited this trait.)

Others present the opposite tendency—they observe more calmly, without fully absorbing or internalizing the scenes. If they interpret actions, they adhere to what is plainly visible—like a child that described a scene by stating, "More children are sitting than standing." This might be considered a realist type, so to speak. Most children fall somewhere in between. They don't bring too much illusionism into what they see.

It is also worth noting that among the twenty or so children who viewed the pictures, six engaged in little more than brief enumeration paired with dry, factual description. They introduced no illusions into the images and were not particularly drawn to them. Anything that might seem fantastical in their descriptions can be attributed to the underdevelopment of perception rather than to the vividness of imagination.

Eidetism and Imagination

In the reproduction of what has been perceived, an interesting phenomenon has been observed in a fairly large number of children, which is particularly prominent in preadolescence and has a significant influence on the spiritual life of the individual. I am referring to eidetic ability. It is necessary to determine whether it plays a role, and to what extent, in a young child's imagination.

Eidetic ability was studied extensively by Erich Rudolf Jaensch and his students. In this work, we will adhere to the explanations presented in Oswald Kroh's study on subjective perceptual images in young boys.[1]

---

1 Oswald Kroh: *Subjektive Anschauungsbilder bei Jugendlichen,* 1922.

Here is what eidetic memory is all about. When describing an object or phenomenon that we have previously seen, we can recount its details in terms of color, shape, and the place where it was seen—though what we "see" with our inner eyes is not the object itself, but only its mental image. As is well known, mental images differ from perceptions in being paler, less corporeal, and more fluid. However, these characteristics vary among individuals. For some, mental images are more vivid and closer to reality, while for others they are dim and lifeless.

It has been observed that certain individuals, when they describe what they have seen, experience the image reappearing before their mind's eye with striking sensual clarity. Whether with their eyes closed or open in a dark environment, they can reproduce the earlier visual impression with a vividness that approaches that of a hallucination. These are subjective images that have the characteristics of perception. They appear in a person's field of vision and are plastic, although they are reproduced with less depth, and are therefore similar to a relief. They often appear in the same colors as the original objects.

Up until the age of fifteen or sixteen, the eidetic type prevails among young people and includes more than half of the subjects in the study who in this case were male children. In many, this eidetic ability is lost with puberty, while in some, it remains throughout life. The decline of this ability lasts for years.

Many artists have eidetic ability, which can play a significant role in the creative process, as it applies to images of the imagination as well as those previously perceived. In artistic creation, as Kroh emphasizes (ibid.), the richness of images, their imaginative qualities, and the esthetic dimensions are more important than likeness or adherence to their sensory source.

Even for non-artists, eidetic images—with their concreteness, fidelity, and status as a special form of visual memory—offer a guarantee of the authenticity of recollections. They bring pleasure by evoking beauty seen long ago and reviving wonderful experiences such as travels.

It should also be added that the appearance of sensual, subjective images often depends on the overall psychological attitude of the individual and his interests. This applies to the deliberate induction of images. However, for young people, spontaneous eidetic imagery is especially characteristic. These images are closely tied to the child's longings and aspirations, often arising in alignment with their interests, for instance, serving as the basis for drawing, writing, or model-making.

While eidetic ability most commonly manifests in the visual domain, it can occur in relation to other senses, even though it is rare. It was necessary to explain about the eidetic ability in general, to better understand its role and significance in early life.

Kroh arrived at his findings by surveying students aged 9 to 19. It must be noted here, that the children of our selected age group cannot be examined in the same direct manner as the older ones, bearing in mind the aims of this study. Instead, conclusions must be drawn through careful observation of their everyday behavior and experiences. But how can we determine whether a young child, when telling a story, is relying on a schematic mental outline or actually experiencing an eidetic image in all its vividness and detail, when he is unable to articulate this distinction? To address this, we must take an indirect approach. There is no claim here that this problem has been fully resolved. Our intention is simply to indicate that this phenomenon—eidetic imagery—can be observed even in preschool-age children.

Describing the development of child's memory, Stern says that from the age of four, memories become more voluminous and more frequent. Individual recollections are no longer isolated fragments, but are instead reproduced in their proper relationships.

This is especially true in the context of spatial memory. A child remembers the topography of an area, the layout of rooms in an apartment, the streets and turns of a familiar route, and the position of people in relation to each other at a particular entrance—sometimes with such clarity and detail that the listener is amazed. At times, these spatial memories are accompanied by distinct topographical movements; the child not only envisions the entire scene, but mentally retraces the same paths. In such cases, visual memory is complemented by motor memory.[1]

Stern supports the facts he presents with examples from children's lives. He goes on to state that at the age of five, it is possible for a child to recall memories from early childhood. A random event can trigger a memory of an experience that happened in the first half of the child's life and had not been recalled until that moment.

Here's an example: Günter, Stern's son (4 years, 6 months) saw the new governess wearing a blue-and-white striped blouse and immediately exclaimed:
"You look like Maria; Maria was wearing such a blouse."
(Two years and three months have passed since Maria left.)
Similarly, Laura Ehrlich, (4 years, 11 months) recently claimed to remember a visit from a relative who had been with the family nearly three years earlier. Stern thought it was impossible for her to remember so much back and questioned her. However, she knew the facts and said:
"The lady of the house was in mourning. We were all sitting in the blue room...." Stern concludes that many impressions, especially visual ones, can

---

1 William Stern: *Psychologie der frühen Kindheit*, 1930, p. 208.

16

have a strikingly unusual effect on young children: "They persist in their form and color with an intensity completely different from that of an adult, possessing an almost hallucinatory power. Even a long period during which they are not recalled—remaining, so to speak, outside of consciousness—does not rob them of their sensory clarity. It is characteristic of all our latest examples that they always retain colors and lights from an age when children do not yet know the names of colors. Thus, the children did not remember the names of the colors, but the colors themselves." Having established these facts, Stern himself notes a resemblance between such phenomena and the eidetic imagery investigated by Erich Rudolf Jaensch and his students.

The later memories of early childhood often possess a hallucinatory quality. According to Stern, they can reach as far back as the second year of life, though they typically consist of isolated moments. Here, again, the sense of sight dominates—these memories are primarily visual in nature. They can be surprising in that an individual may carry them internally for a long time, unnoticed even by the individual himself, until they unexpectedly resurface with varying degrees of clarity. These mental images owe their permanence and persistence to their emotional significance. The reason certain experiences remain preserved in memory is that they were shaped by strong feelings or a particular interest.[1]

I have chosen this approach to present concrete facts demonstrating that eidetic ability exists early in life. Similar examples can be found in other psychological studies focused on this stage of development. An alternative approach would be to attempt to explain the genesis of eidetic ability and thus to develop a theory of this phenomenon.

That is the approach taken by Kroh. However, it does not seem to me that such a theory would hold greater significance for our purposes or provide more insight into this phenomenon than Stern's observations. Instead, we will supplement Stern's findings with those of Kroh whenever they offer broader or more compelling support for the conclusions drawn from Stern's work.

Before anything else, I will draw from my own experience. Kroh claims that the fact that the eidetic ability once existed is eventually forgotten. Perhaps this is true in most cases, but it is not in mine. I retained this trait even when I was no longer very young, besides, it brought me so much pleasure in childhood that I can never completely forget it.

Some might argue that my memory of this ability is merely a construction—an invention shaped by imagination over time. But I see no reason to place greater trust in the assumptions of others than in my own

---

1 William Stern: *Psychology der frühen Kindheit*, 1930, p. 212.

lived experience. Moreover, I noted with sadness the disappearance of this ability and carry within me a deep awareness of the distinction between both types of mental representation. I should add that I did not notice when the change occurred, but one day I suddenly realized that I no longer possessed this ability.

My first memory dates back to my second year of life. When I first shared it with my mother, I was still very young. She was initially surprised and listened with disbelief, trying to attribute it to something I might have heard from her or others. Yet, each time I spoke about that event, a vivid image would rise before me—full of light and color, rich in details that no one's retelling could have conveyed with such plasticity and vividness.

Even then, for me, that very vividness—this ability to see subtle nuances of color—was a sign that I was carrying within me a true image of reality. Today, when I recall that same experience, it exists in my mind almost solely as a verbal memory. Compared to my earlier recollection it now feels like a pencil drawing whose sharp contours have been partially erased by time—some areas remain distinct, while others have faded in contrast to the once-vivid picture full of bright colors and flickering light.

"I see before me tables placed-together, covered with shiny white tablecloths. Candles glow. The room full of light. Around me, many smiling, happy faces. Suddenly those faces rise and quickly flee. Someone is carrying me. We reach a balcony where we see a wooden railing. We descend the stairs into the night. The person carrying me stops at the door of a small house and sets me down for a moment. I can see inside a small room with a dirt floor. Blood. A pile of broken bottles whose shards glisten with a greenish-blue sheen covers the corpse of a woman. They carry me again. We pass by something that brushes against us with its leaves. Not a soul around us. The image stops."

It was an experience of a pogrom.

Evidently, it is an image full of liveliness. I cite it because it supports Stern's view that memories from that age are affectively induced. The contrasts of that evening were so stark that they left traces in my mind—like an image imprinted on a photographic plate—before I was even capable of fully understanding them.

Joyful, cheerful people, a brightly lit room; later, the sudden escape, blood, a corpse, and finally, the silence of the night—I believe these contrasts explain the depth of the impression. But perhaps an early sensitivity to color also played a role. In this memory, color matters. It carries weight.

I used to carry within me several such plastic images from early childhood, originating from various years. It seems to me that these events etched themselves into my memory because they were tied to certain childhood wishes and emotional states triggered by new situations—for example, a walk taken on my own, or something similar. All those things, so minor to an adult, must have held the significance of a powerful experience back then.

Kroh maintains that in an early phase of development, an eidetic image should be regarded as the primary manifestation of memory. My own recollections seem to confirm his findings. He writes:

"There can be no doubt that the memory phenomena of the type represented by extremely vivid, concrete images must be considered particularly suited to the child's mental state. A mere internal representation, the production of which requires an unnaturally high degree of attention withdrawal from peripheral stimuli—something unlikely in a child—cannot be regarded as a suitable vehicle for a child's memory activity. In contrast, a true image to which the child can direct his almost exclusively sensory attention, allows for prolonged observation. This attention, with its sensitivity and resemblance to examination, is undoubtedly better suited to the child's psychological development. The result of this interpretation of memory is a new approach that encourages the analysis of individual parts while also fostering an understanding of the whole complex of child's memory."[1]

If this understanding is adopted, it would explain why the memory images of youth are largely vivid and plastic. The field studies conducted by Ressk also emphasize the strong presence of concreteness in children's imagery. He found that the mental representations formed by the young mind differ significantly from those of adults—that purely internal representations still retain perceptual vividness (at least in certain details), and that such representations remain characteristic of the mind until approximately the age of fifteen.

Similarly, E. Meumann observes that a young person lives in a world of imagination that is much closer to sensory experience than to abstract, word-based thinking.[2]

Here we find a partial agreement with the facts mentioned above. However, eidetic ability is not limited to enhancing memory plasticity, thus contributing to a child's overall development. It also plays a significant role in the function of a child's imagination.

Kroh (ibid. paragraph 9) presents his findings on the eidetic type among students. We encounter children aged 11 and 12 as writers of compositions, storytellers who entertain their peers with fictional stories, and inventors of machines based on their eidetic images, all the while envisioning their future

---

1 Kroh: *Subjektive Anschauungsbilder bei Jugendlichen*, 1922, pp.120-121.

2 E. Meumann: *Vorlesungen zu Einführung in die experimentelle Pädagogik, 1 Band*, 1916, p. 512.

lives. This suggests that the eidetic disposition offers an abundance of material for the imagination, providing it with concrete and plastic images.

If we assume that we have indeed succeeded in identifying the existence of eidetic images in early life—and we hope this is the case—the manner in which the mind later utilizes this faculty at a higher level will allow us to extend these findings to the age group we are interested in. More mature individuals place eidetic images at the service of their imagination, guided by their interests, whether in creative pursuits or simple leisure activities.

The children in the age group we are discussing in this book are primarily interested in play. They play with objects, movements, and language. They will certainly play with the eidetic images available to them. When their imagination is absorbed in play, inventing stories, or attempting to make sense of the world, these activities often involve weaving together images.

I can confirm this from my own experience, which I still remember clearly. It happened in my seventh or eighth year of life, therefore slightly later than the age of the children we are focusing on here. Reflecting on my own earlier experiences, I can affirm that playing with eidetic images enables the imagination to build upon them. More broadly, the entire process of invention tends to rely on such images.

Playing with eidetic images is also closely connected to child's engagement with hearing and interpreting fairy tales. Despite their naturally active nature, children are capable of calmly listening to fairy tales and becoming immersed in their imaginary world. These are not just fleeting words that pass by and randomly arrange themselves in the child's mind. Rather, they evoke vivid images—sometimes sharp, sometimes more diffuse—that unroll before the child's inner eye and remain fresh long after many newer experiences have faded.

More about fairy tales will be discussed elsewhere. Adults close to the child often cannot perceive what lies behind the child's stories and gestures; to them, it must seem like mere fiction when a child, walking through a meadow, exclaims that he sees many tiny people dressed in red and blue promenading across the grass—while they see only flowers and greenery.

Similarly, it might seem like a fabrication when a child returns home from an outing and claims to have seen a wolf. Yet such statements are often revived details from the fairy tales or other memories, shaped by eidetic experiences and projected onto the outside world. In such moments, the child is not lying but engaging in imaginative play, in which memory and perception blend freely. Here, imagination combines past memories with new experiences to form original scenarios, revealing another key feature of children's fantasy: its combinatory role.

Combinatory Ability

The creation of new works depends on the combinatory capacity of the imagination. In adult creations, the process of combining, that is the joining of given parts into a new whole, proceeds toward a specific goal. This guiding idea determines the direction of the imagination's representations, ensuring that the creation, no matter how complex, feels like a whole. Let us now examine how a child's imagination functions in this regard. In doing so, the most material will come from children's conversations and storytelling that arises spontaneously during play, drawing, or other activities.

First, I will translate from German the greater part of the monologue spoken by Ludwig Strümpell's[1] daughter (1 year, 9 months), as cited by Karl Groos in his work *Das Seelenleben des Kindes*.

> "Bed, lie down, darling Teoduja (Teoduza is the name of her doll),
> golden dream bring Teoduja
> run, tap, tap, tap around
> strawberries, grandma, wolf
> bed, lie down, sleep
> sleep Teoduja, my heart, you are my dearest
> everything sleeps, quiet, zz, zz
> dear May, make trees green again, make violets bloom by the creek
> I would like go walk
> cat comes in
> mother takes it on her lap, cat has legs, black boots…." and so on.

As one can see, this is a rather lengthy monologue that lacks the structure to connect its parts toward a specific purpose. The words come spontaneously— one triggering the next—while two or three may form small phrases, carry a special meaning, and stand out from the rest. There are leaps from scene to scene, or transitions from one small unit to another, where a word or a sound redirects the flow. These shifts are often interwoven with fragments of familiar songs, stories, or personal associations.There is no clear thread, no synthesis holding the whole together.

Herein lies an important distinction between creative imagination and this early expression of a very young child's imagination: what we witness here is an unconscious creation—if we may call it that—because it is purely instinctive, much like the kicking of little legs and arms. The child surrenders wholly to imagination. One utterance follows another through simple association, without guidance of will. Unlike adult creativity, the child does not select among images which float before his eyes, or return to a unifying purpose.The process is unfiltered and free of intent.

Occasionally, even in a small child, one can observe a tendency to form a cohesive whole. This tendency is usually so short-lived that it includes only fragments of

---

1 Ludwig Adolf Strümpell: *Psychologische Pädagogik*, 1880, p.169.

a story, and so weak that whatever elements appear during the performance—whether a similarity of sounds, or spatial or temporal relationships—can associatively change the direction of the story as it unfolds (Stern).

I will cite one of Stern's examples, quoting his daughter Hilda (age 3), as it illustrates a characteristic way in which a young child connects scenes within a story.

In this case, everything that came to her mind revolved around chickens. The element that ties the pieces together is the chicken coop.

> Hilda: "And then the chicken coop door closed, and then the hens themselves lay down, closed their eyes, and slept soundly. But look, then came a big chair (she had just bumped into the chair) and the hens sat on it. (Mother: Ah!) Well, yes, then they also got such a book for their birthday... Look at the hens' stove, the chicks lit it. They brought wood and coal from the kitchen, and even the little box with the candles in it. (She uses this description instead of the word 'matchbox,' which she doesn't yet use.)
> Then the rooster lit the light. Father rooster and Mother hen—what will they do today? (She clearly didn't yet know what to do with them herself.)
> Today they will sit at the table and eat soup."

This example illustrates how fragile the flow of a young child's imagination can be and how easily it changes direction depending on impressions of the surrounding world, his memories, and his knowledge of things. At the same time, it is clear that the child is not taking into account whether the details of the story fit into a coherent whole. Alongside this characteristic way in which children link representations—marked by meandering and instability—children's imagination also possesses an opposite trait.

A young child can repeat the same word or the same movement many times without feeling bored by the monotony of action, instead performing it with the same original enthusiasm. This phenomenon is known as **perseveration**. I am standing next to a child who is waiting for the tram with his mother. As the tram approaches from a distance, the child sings, I don't know how many times, a melody he has "composed" himself:

"There comes the dear tram," he sings and waves to it with his free little hand, while the other clutches a small pail for watering flowers.

A child can listen to the same story and repeat the same verses with a tenacity and patience we, as adults, rarely possess. Thus, in the combinatory work of a child's imagination, we find, side by side, both fleeting liveliness and the monotony of repetition. These seemingly opposite qualities coexist in children's storytelling.

The younger the child, the more the self stands at the center of his imagination. This connection between the self and imagination is either direct—the child inserts himself into the event—or indirect, by introducing personal details into the story, retelling something he has heard, or reimagining a scene he has observed. This is illustrated by the following example:

> Mara (3 years, 6 months) reads, holding a piece of paper with some writing on it: "Dear Mara, you are good. Our village has gathered. Mara kisses her sweetheart." (This relates to the song: 'Mara has, Mara has…') At 3 o'clock, come to Mara's for the ironing (apparently a village activity), and let the little girls play."

This example illustrates how the children's imagination ties different elements together, but it also shows that Mara is at the center of everything. This is reminiscent of the phenomenon observed already in young children when viewing pictures: Their previous experiences seem to overpower what they are looking at. The image serves to evoke the child's own experiences. This style of children's storytelling seems to confirm the egocentric nature of their thinking.

To study the combinatory work of a child's imagination, I chose to work with the same children who had previously interpreted images in picture books. Here is how I proceeded:

First, I introduced the activity as a new kind of a game, getting the children used to guessing the ending of a story as soon as I told it. These were short stories with few details. Since a circus had recently come to town, I took that into account and told the children a story about a little frog who goes to the circus. Each child was then asked to imagine and tell me their own ending to the story. This narrative included only one main character—the frog—on which their imagination had to focus.

Another example involved a girl, a doll, a dog, and a sudden downpour of rain. This story, too, required the children to invent an ending. The story about the frog and the circus seemed much closer to the children's heart, perhaps because the arrival of the circus was a major event for them.

The children repeated the story two or three times: first, immediately after my narration, and then again several days later. In the initial retelling, immediate memory could have played a greater role, with combinatory activity serving mainly to invent an ending. However, in the second or third round, I assume that forgetting the story line could have encouraged the children to recombine its elements into a new whole. In the first round, memory was more dominant, while combinatory activity had not yet fully shaped the ending. In later retellings, forgetting certain details allowed for greater creative recombination.

In the case of the youngest child (4 years old), the combination is primarily expressed through repetition of the same action:

"The frog went. The circus came. The frog went to the circus and saw a pony." In the spirit of the previous examples, the same terms are sequenced repeatedly without synthesis. The only notable addition is: "He saw a pony."

It is likely that the pony was his favorite part of the circus, which is why he included that detail.

The story told by another boy (5 years, 1 month) is interesting because he directly incorporates elements of his own life into the narrative. However, he loses sight of the original storyline and instead strings together a series of associations—some based on what he knows about frogs, others drawn from personal experience. He narrates:

> "There was a frog, and she came out of the river. She watched the circus and saw the ponies. So she went into the hole, then she fell down and went underground. She wiped herself with a towel, got dressed, and went to sleep. So she got some sleep. Then she got more sleep and then went to play."

Most of the other children, however, shaped the story into a complete whole with a brand-new ending, as instructed. Here, I would like to remind you of my earlier observation when examining the pictures: even at this stage of development, children display the unique character of their imagination. Some move away from reality, losing sight of it entirely, while others conclude the story in a highly realistic manner. In the following examples, we can see how a child perceives reality and is influenced by it.

> A seven-year-old girl said:
> "I think she (the frog) was run over by a car and croaked."
> A five-year-old girl said:
> "She liked watching the show. When it was over, she went home."
> A six-and-a-half year old boy:
> "She went and watched the show every day. Then she went to look again.Then the frog died because someone stepped on her."

Here are a few examples that show a greater immersion in the story:

> A six-year-old boy: "She goes, she goes, and sees the circus. She watched the performance of that guy—probably some performer. She danced in the circus."

Another example seems to carry a cautionary message:

> "The frog went home and told her mom what she saw. Mom said, 'Don't go there alone, they'll step on you.' She went alone, watched the circus. They stepped on her."

It is interesting to observe how the story evolved and became more complete after a few days. It was as if the imagination had time to deepen and refine its work, while memory solidified and retained certain details. Besides, the way the story was told now revealed more of he little storyteller's personality. This is how the five-year-old girl recounted the story the second time:

> "When it was night, she couldn't go home. She went to the door and then a bear came at her and ate her up."

A 7-year-old girl: "One evening she (the frog) saw a circus. She was little. She looked and wondered what this big, big thing was. Later, her mother also went and looked."

The repetition of "big, big" and other similar words she used during the conversation seems to be a characteristic feature of a child's speech. I believe that by repeating the same attribute to emphasize the importance of what she was describing, the young narrator was attempting to underline her sense of admiration for this unknown, immense thing that had suddenly appeared in front of her. In this context, the repetition is no longer mere enumeration or perseveration; rather, it serves an emotional purpose and reflects the child's deep immersion in the experience.

I deliberately separated the results obtained from the second story—about a girl, a doll, and a dog—and here is why: During the conversation, one must keep track of all three elements simultaneously. This appears to exceed the cognitive capacity of children aged 4 to 7. Only a small number of children were able to remember all three elements throughout the story; some followed them only for part of the narrative, while others lost sight of the protagonists entirely.

The story is about a little girl who has a doll and a dog. She is outside in the yard when it starts to rain. She forgets her playmates and runs into the house. The task for the children was to describe how the event ended. That same day, while my story was still fresh in their minds, I asked twelve children who had participated to complete it.

The results were as follows:

Zagorka (7 years old) described the ending in a way that completely confirmed my perception of her:

"I think the rain fell and carried away the doll. Then the dog took it out, then brought it back. After that the little girl played with her doll."

Here we see the imagination that remains grounded in both the task and in reality.

The second girl, who is the same age, includes all three characters but she introduces some changes—having the girl take the doll into the house with her, while the dog returns later on its own.

A boy (6 years, 6 months) unintentionally blends this story with another, transforming the dolly into a child who saves a dog. He shifts from one storyline to another without realizing it, yet manages to maintain all three roles until the end.

Another boy (6 years, 8 months) also retains all three characters until the end, but divides the story into two parts, each involving only two characters at a time. I believe it will not be uninteresting to present his "composition."

"The girl left the dog outside and it rained on him. She ran inside. When the rain stopped, she went out and played with the children. After that, she played with the doll. It rained again. She ran inside.

It was raining on the little dog. And the dog froze. He asked to be let inside to warm up."

Nada (5 years, 1 month) loses track of the dog but connects the little girl to her doll in a touching way:

"When the rain returned, the girl ran inside. The paint on the doll was washed off. The little girl cried."

It is obvious that the child is genuinely engaged with the situation and demonstrates an understanding of the reality.

Our little 4-year-old friend also forgets about the dog, but we can not say that he simply stacks events one after another because he uses one role to connect to the others. This is how he does it:

"She played with the doll near the river. It was raining heavily. She ran into the house, fell into the river, and they pulled her out. After that she didn't want to play near the river any more."

Two more children created stories in which they combined two of the three elements. The rest focused solely on the girl from the beginning, and spoke only of her.

The story told by Velibor (6 years, 6 months) is a particularly characteristic case. He also, to begin with, loses sight of the dog and the doll, and keeps only the girl, but every now and then he introduces into his story another hero, who appears and disappears across a sequence of fluid, dreamlike scenes that unfold as if they might never end:

"When it rained, she ran into the house. And it rained inside the house. Then Grandfather came in from town, and they built a big two-story house and sat there. After that, they sat there for a long time. Grandfather was a merchant, so he was giving the girl some money, and they bought everything for lunch.They stayed there for a long time. The little room fell in but the big one didn't.
Grandfather died. That little girl wailed, and wailed, and then she died from crying. The house remained empty. Later, the owner came and he got married. They sat for a long time, then a male child was born, then a female child."

I asked him if the story is over. He replied: "I don't know." In this way, the conversation could have continued for as long as we wanted—his source of inventing stories is inexhaustible. I wanted to see whether he realized that this was not the story I had in mind. When I asked him about it, he immediately understood that he did not fulfill the task, so another, possibly even livelier version is born:

"They go for a walk (the girl and the dog). She teaches the dog to beg, so the dog goes and begs. Then, when it gets dark, they go home together. And then an angel comes and protects them. When the angel comes, everything is glowing.The father and mother don't see the angel. When the people in the house wake up, the mother comes and sees all the gold. That's how God taught the puppies how to beg."

As he speaks, his eyes are alive and animated—his voice as well. He follows everything with movement. And despite all the twists and turns of his imagination, there is no trace of nonsense. A central idea binds a greater or lesser part of his stories into a whole. The transitions are smooth: when the girl dies, the house is left empty, so it feels natural that others move in. He also touches on emotional states, as in the line: "The girl dies from crying."

It is characteristic that as soon as one chain of events gets interrupted at its starting point, another begins to take shape. This suggests an imagination so lively that it can barely wait to be set in motion. Although in this case, the stimulus for imagination was triggered by an assignment, the child's inventiveness does not differ in any way from the spontaneous children's stories which Stern refers to as **fabulations**. The child's imagination here does not seem constrained by the task in any way; rather, the assignment merely serves as a springboard for the child to begin creating. One can sense his desire to imbue the story with the same unusual quality of wonder and strangeness that children delight in when listening to fairy tales.

"When the angel came, everything was glowing." In his way of inventing and interpreting the images he envisions—so different from the approach of other children in his group—we see a child with a very vivid and relatively rich imagination. This is a child who does not receive any special attention, as he comes from a family of modest means. After all, the vividness of imagination expressed in children's stories, inventions, and games has little to do with external influences.

Unfortunately, only five children retold this story for the second time. The same children who left some characters out of the story the first time did so again. However, the second performance was better than the first, as if the material solidified. This supports the observations drawn from the first story. After a few days, the elements of subsequent memory begin to emerge. In other words, details that were initially overlooked now come to the surface. The child, who had previously vacillated between two or three elements now provides a complete story, from which the doll has completely disappeared. Even the little four-year-old includes all three characters again, producing a well-formed narrative.

"The little girl had a doll and played with both the doll and the dog. She went inside because it was raining. Then she didn't want to play anymore. Both the doll and the dog got all wet."

Regardless of how these three elements are arranged, it is characteristic that most children between ages 4 and 7 struggle to retain them in their minds for long and account for them until the end of the story. This brief narrative only confirms that the role of will and attention in the creative work of imagination is still weak at this stage. The task either fades early on or remains only as a partial goal.

Here, we can observe the individual nature of imagination. Some children give their story realistic features, as the one who said that the color got washed off. Others add their own ideas and introduce fantastic elements. In one case, when the rain stops, the girl's mother and father suddenly disappear, leaving her alone and crying. These differences lead us to the same conclusions as when analyzing children's drawings, namely, that even at this early stage of life, imagination varies significantly among individuals. This variation is not only a mater of how vivid the imagination is, but it also reflects the child's overall attitude. One child may focus more on reality, while another follows his feelings, creating new combinations that express inner experiences regardless of how closely they align with the real world.

The common features of children's combinatory storytelling can be described as follows: To begin with, when observing the imaginative combinations of younger children, it becomes clear that they are incapable of true synthesis. The working of imagination appears disjointed and arbitrary, marked by frequent shifts in attention from one scene to another. There is also a tendency toward perseveration, where certain sequences are repeated, but even in these repetitions, no real synthesis occurs. In these young storytellers' combinations, the "I" or "self" plays a prominent role. The children often insert themselves directly into the story, placing themselves at its center (as in the stories of Ljerka and Mara). Alternatively, the stories provide details which fit their lifestyles, as in the tale of the frog, told by nursery school children aged 4 and 5.

As development progresses, imagination becomes increasingly guided by the will, making its workings less whimsical. The child gains the ability to create more complete narratives. Coupled with the strengthening of this intentional aspect of imagination, there is also a developing awareness of the task at hand, provided it is not too difficult for the child. This growth happens gradually. Even among children aged 6 or 7, this awareness can sometimes fade in the face of the lively flow of unfolding scenes. As a result, for many children, the task serves merely as a trigger for imagination, rather than a strict guideline. With the emergence of synthesis in their combinative work, children also develop an urge to express their feelings through a specific way of talking. They may repeat a single word, attribute, or action to emphasize its importance. In doing so, the child follows his emotions, using repetition to highlight the importance of a particular moment in time. In the previously mentioned work, Groos discusses two additional forms of combination in children's imagination.

The first such form is the **magnification and diminution** of certain characteristics of objects. Groos finds that the transition to true imaginative activity in this sense involves **deliberate exaggeration**, especially in cases when the child's interest in what is incredible or striking goes along with a sense of self-importance connected to the supposed experience or possession of something extreme. "I have thirty marbles—no, fifty—no, a hundred—no, a thousand!"

This tendency toward exaggeration also appears in the creations of children's imagination, even when unrelated to personal experience. For example, Groos's little daughter, when she was five and a half years old, improvised a story by pretending to read a fairy tale from a book:

> "Once upon a time there was a king who had a little daughter. The little daughter was lying in the cradle. The king came over and realized that she was his daughter. Then the two of them had a wedding. While they were sitting at the table, the king asked her to bring him a large glass of beer. So, she brought a cup that was thirty yards tall. Then everyone fell asleep; only the king remained awake as a watchman. And if they did not die, they are still alive today."

The second phenomenon consists in the **separation** of some of the features from the way they are usually connected, and their transfer to another entity. This (just like an urge to exaggerate) is not a specific phenomenon of a child's imagination, but it is important that it appears early in the productive work of fantasy. Thus, at the end of the fifth year, Groos's daughter spoke to her doll like this:

> "So, little sister Olga, are you coming home from a walk? Tell me, what did you see out there?"
> "A little sheep, a cow, a dog, a horse." "Yes, and what else?"
> "A little blue bluebell, green patches of lungwort, red leaves."
> "But those don't grow there—you are lying, my little sister!"

At this stage of development, a child does not yet have fully formed understanding of size, colors and other qualities of objects, but he is in the process of acquiring them. Still, exaggeration cannot be explained by this alone. This tendency—along with the ability to separate and recombine elements—brings great pleasure to the child and stems from a desire for the unusual, which finds expression in this playful form of storytelling.

Now that we have explored the combinative capability of young children, the question arises: can we also nurture it, and if so, how? With general development, the child's imagination also grows stronger. It is therefore important to provide opportunities to experience various activities that enrich the mind. Contact with nature has an exceptionally beneficial effect. It offers the child a wide range of sensory impressions, which he absorbs and interprets according to his intellectual capacity. Walking across open fields, for example, combined with thoughtful conversation about the natural phenomena that spark his interest, positively impacts both his body and mind. On the other hand, if the child's environment lacks stimulation—if he is confined to the same gray, miserable backyard with no grass and flowers, or where the walls block the view, his spirit will lack fuel, and his body will lack space and opportunity for movement. The impressions and experiences the child gathers are later reflected in his play. He will speak of them to his toys or to other children, draw them, or relive them through other forms of imaginative expression.

At this stage of life, more than at any other, the intentional influence of an educator must follow the path marked by nature, if it is to be truly effective. It is essential to give children opportunities for meaningful experiences at an early age, along with the tools to express them. The educator's primary task should be to select carefully the influences to which the child is exposed. The child's creative imagination will reveal itself through the combinatory activities that emerge in play. At times, a child may welcome gentle guidance in arranging trees and blocks or choosing which models to build, based on foundations we provide. However, even when we intervene, we must do so by closely following the wishes of the child, and our behavior must remain in the spirit of play.

Thus, the development of child's combinatory ability is primarily achieved through play. In the form of play, the child engages with whatever captures his interest and seeks to express it. At preschool age, the child gives expression to everything that interests him, everything he wishes to convey. Under "play" we include here all forms of expression characteristic of the preschool period. However, it is also possible to influence the ability to combine more directly. For this purpose, Meumann[1] recommends for younger children the use of **Heilbronner method**, which involves having them interpret schematic images which gradually become more complete.

Fig. 1 is one such example (see p. 31) of a progressively more complex schema supplied by William Stern in his *Psychologie der Frühen Kindheit: Tafelanhang, Tafel.II.*

Any method that encourages the child to freely combine several ingredients to create a coherent whole or a well-rounded thought is beneficial. Meumann, (ibid. p. 535) quotes an example by Janet Masselon who provides various combinations of three words that serve to form a sentence.

Combinatory ability can also be developed by giving the children the beginning—or a substantial part—of a story and asking them to complete it on their own. It is essential that such tasks match the child's stage of development. If we adjust them in respect to the child's maturity and understanding, these exercises can be successfully used even with very young children.

---

1 Ernst Meumann: *Vorlesungen zur Einführung in die experimentelle Pädagogik,* I Band, 1916, p. 524.

Fig. 1

According to Meumann, studies have shown that memorizing stories also increases child's ability to compose stories.

All these activities encourage independent work of the imagination, which is where their true value lies. Naturally, the format of these tasks must be appropriate for early childhood. Everything should feel like a game to a small child, so that he happily engages in these tasks.

At this early age, the role of imagination is immense. It pervades the entire life of the child, although its intensity varies from one child to another. Later, its scope becomes more limited, as individual differences emerge which determine the direction of its productivity. No matter what means we use, we cannot develop imagination beyond the strength of a child's natural disposition. However, with the right approach, we can help it reach its fullest potential. That is why it is essential to cultivate imagination in childhood—so it may serve the individual not only in early years but throughout life, fostering both an appreciation of art and the ability to create within the limits of one's innate abilities.

THE CAREFREENESS
OF CHILD'S IMAGINATION

Having examined both aspects of children's imagination—its illusionistic quality and its combinative activity—we will now compare them by focusing on their general characteristics rather than on the specific differences revealed through closer analysis.

We have seen that children's imagination displays a strong tendency toward **illusionism**, especially in younger children. In this sense, it resembles artistic imagination, as it enriches child's experiences by lifting them beyond the narrow constraints of everyday life into a broader, more imaginative world. Through this ability, children create new forms, reshape their environment, and transform their experiences. In short, illusionism enables them to interpret reality, especially during early childhood, when play is their primary mode of engagement.

The combinatory function of imagination, in its early stages, is characterized by the ease with which its elements can be rearranged, often without true synthesis. The advent of synthesis manifests itself as a characteristic of further development. The subjective elements also enter the combinatory work of imagination, especially at first. As children develop a greater understanding of unity and coherence, they supply the details according to their personal experiences, without worrying whether they make sense in regard to the same unity. They do not concern themselves with the agreement between reality and their representation of it. In productive, or more precisely, combinatory imagination, they do not always ensure that the elements they combine form a meaningful or coherent whole.

Stern states that the child does not care at all what kind of object his imagination is attached to. No matter how random the shape of a torn piece of paper, a child may declare it a "shoe" even though, to our eyes, there is only a distant resemblance between the two. There is almost no connection between the horse and the stick on which the boy rides, says Stern. The fact that the stick can be placed between the legs is enough to realize the working of imagination. Stern calls this feature of imagination **carefreeness**. It is marked by the indifference of a child's imagination to the external form of objects he is engaged with.

One can see the advantage of being in such a state, as it promotes liveliness with which life is played out in a child's imagination. This freedom is made possible, explains Stern, by the relative meagerness of the presented object. If a small child truly needed to deal with a distinct idea of the shape and color of a shoe, then a glance at a piece of paper could not so easily lead him to interpret it as one. The lack of specific elements in the piece of paper that deviate from the appearance of a shoe allows the child to reach this conclusion without hesitation.

Interpreting a stick as a riding horse does not bother the little rider because, compared to the main attribute of a horse—its rideability—all other features, especially the horse's size and shape, withdraw completely into the background. The child wants to move quickly from scene to scene, from action to action, and that is why it suffices to isolate a single appealing feature of an object that he likes and make it the backbone of his motor activity. This explains how the same object can, at different moments, serve as a stimulus for imagining entirely different things.

If we remember that even at the beginning of the second year of life, a child can recognize the familiar faces in small pictures, as Kroh aptly points out, then the above explanation about children's representations of insufficiently clear contours and colors becomes less convincing. Furthermore, if we take into account previously mentioned fact—that the first childhood memories resemble some photographic images in which most objects retain their colors and lighting—and that some such memories are already possible from the second year of life, then the discrepancy in the Stern's theory will appear even greater.

In light of this, an alternative explanation comes to mind: The child draws upon the similarities of different objects because, where an adult perceives only faint traces of resemblance, the child's eidetic capability allows him to recognize genuine similarities, blending the eidetic image with the actual one. In this process, the subjective image fuses with the perception of the real object. In other words, the illusionism of the child's imagination plays a role here, and the child's apparent "indifference" to the actual form of the object is a result of this merging between imagination and perception.

When, in the course of further development, the child comes to understand the difference between the subjective and the objective—when he gradually masters his illusionism (and we have seen that he vacillates in this respect throughout the entire phase we are dealing with)—then he becomes more aware of the distinction between the object that inspires his fantasy and its representation. At this point, the object becomes a **symbol** for what his imagination needs. For example, a child may take pebbles to represent the grazing cows or, perhaps, the children at play, assigning each a role and speaking on behalf of every imagined child.

The child engaged in such play is aware of what the objects he is playing with really are, but this knowledge recedes into the background. It is as if the objects themselves gradually fade from view, while the meaning assigned to them within the game takes precedence. This creates a kind of doubling of consciousness: during the game, the symbolic meaning of the object becomes more prominent than its real-world identity. A comparison with an actor comes to mind—the child immerses himself in the chosen role and in the objects involved in play, focusing more on the imaginative role than on objective reality. Once again, the child's indifference to the real meaning of the object is evident—although now, at a higher level, he is fully aware of it.

Considering another aspect of the child's imaginative activity, we have seen that, early on, a desire emerges to combine the smaller elements into the larger relationships. For children, however, combining mostly means surrendering to the flow of the narrative.

Later, even when the child is capable of forming small wholes, a certain tendency persists to favor individual parts over the overall structure. The selections often highlight details that, from an adult's perspective, do not belong in the larger context. (The little narrator tells us that the child drowned in the river but later still went home.)

We might attribute this to a younger child's limited ability to **synthesize**. Yet, even in such cases, there is a marked disregard for coherent narrative construction and a certain indifference toward the kind of product imagination ultimately yields.

There is also an unconscious incorporation of elements from the child's own life into the product of imagination, which characterizes the combinatory nature of a child's creativity. This process exhibits the same indifference to the possible and the impossible. Here, also, the child's capacity for illusion allows him to perceive things differently from how they actually appear, and to change that appearance according to his imaginative illusion. The scenes he combines serve a single purpose: they exist for his play. That is why the child does not relate to his creations like an artist does, observing them from the outside. An artist maintains a dual stance: on one hand, the creator; on the other, a critical observer who evaluates the work. The child is fully immersed in the act of creation, working from within and unable to step back to examine the result critically.

He not only cannot watch himself creating—he simply does not attempt to—because the selection and sequencing of scenes unfolds in the way that pleases him. In both cases, imagination functions the same way: It serves the individual by making creativity possible. These phenomena can be understood through the lens of the child's egocentrism which underlies them all.

If we speak about the similarity between the child's and adult's creative artistic imagination in terms of illusionism, we should also point out here the difference that stems from their very different modes of creation.

The artist's activity is guided by the thought or idea to which he wants to give form. The creative process is directed toward an outcome that will best fit the original vision—it is a means to achieve a specific purpose.

For the child, however, it is the process itself that holds the greatest importance. The child tells stories, draws, and plays primarily for the joy inherent in the activity itself. Although the child's imagination may follow a self-imposed task, he is the one who creates that task and pours himself into it, because the act of creating is intrinsically pleasurable. The creator's relationship to his work is deeply personal, as he experiences joy or disappointment based on the outcome.

A child is not as deeply attached to his work as an adult artist might be. He is delighted when he successfully draws or creates something and proudly shows it to those around him. He might even keep it for a while, but when the need arises during play, he happily uses the same finished product for another purpose, especially in the case of visual creations. His stories and ideas often serve only an immediate need, and are quickly forgotten.

As we can see, both the literary and artistic expressions of a child's imagination share a common trait. This is entirely natural, for just as a person's individuality emerges through every activity, so too must each stage of life have characteristic features that color everything it touches.

FAIRY TALE AND THE STORIES CHILDREN INVENT

About Fairy Tales

Children develop a desire to hear stories quite early in life. It is well known that, at times, their need for storytelling and explanation is as strong as their need to play. They want to know about everything—this thing, that picture, and all that surrounds them. When a story is tailored to their level of understanding, they listen intently following the story's twists and turns with their whole being. These little ones, usually so full of movement, sit quietly in such moments, their entire focus evident on their faces—an expression that reveals a withdrawal from the surrounding world and complete immersion in the one conjured by the narrator. That a child asks for a story and becomes so captivated by it suggests that this activity satisfies some deep inner need. A child's craving for fairy tales is closely tied to the illusionism and other characteristics of his imagination, making it a subject worthy of deeper examination.

Children's educators—most often a mother—invent stories for children, adapt familiar ones, and skillfully use them as tools for education. This reflects not only a desire to please a child but also an intuitive understanding of the importance of storytelling. The child's request for a story underscores his need to employ his imagination and enrich his life. This marks the beginning of the same longing that later drives us, as adults, to read novels, listen to folk songs, watch theatre performances, and so on—depending on our level of spiritual development and personal interest. It is this longing that inspires creativity and enables us to appreciate what belongs to the realm of beauty. Therefore, the story must be adjusted to suit the child, otherwise it cannot affect him or satisfy his vibrant inner need.

Young children are usually told fairy tales. This type of literature captivates them and is perhaps listened to with more dedication and enthusiasm then adults exhibit when they read some famous, interesting novel or watch a world-renown theater play. A child's love for fairy tales suggests an intimate connection with them—one that aligns closely with the needs of the developing imagination. A psychological analysis of the fairy tale, therefore, offers a valuable opportunity to explore the nature and characteristics of children's imaginative life.

Charlotte Bühler follows the same approach when she studies children's imagination.[1] Her *Fairy Tale and Child's Imagination* is a beautiful study focused on Grimm's fairy tales which are often the first literature introduced to children in Germany.

---

1 Charlotte Bühler: *Das Märchen und die Phantasie des Kindes*, 1929.

Today, the fairy tales collected by the Grimm brothers are among the most beloved children's literature in the world, not only in Germany. They are a household staple in Serbia as well. In some regions, these stories feel so familiar that people consider them part of their own folk tradition. *Little Red Riding Hood*, *The Wolf and the Seven Little Kids*, *Snow White*, and many others, are cherished companions to our children from early childhood.

An analysis of these fairy tales reveals why these characters are so dear to children in general and why the fairy tales—especially those collected by the Grimm brothers—have become essential literature for young children. I will explore the relationship between the child's imagination and the fairy tale, largely through Charlotte Bühler's analysis mentioned above. Where appropriate, I will connect this analysis with themes discussed in the previous chapter. Thus, this discussion will not be limited strictly to the psychological analysis of the fairy tales.

To strongly emphasize the uniqueness of the fairy tale period, we will, as Bühler did, touch on the time that precedes it and the period that follows. From fairy tales, the child gradually transitions to books whose heroes are characterized by strength, diligence, and wisdom. At that age, our children particularly love folk songs and stories about legendary heroes. They take great interest in hearing detailed accounts of where and how these heroes accomplish their deeds. They are fascinated by traveling to unknown places, making discoveries, and dealing with difficult situations. Bühler calls this stage the period of 'Robinson Crusoe,' named after the novel that remains one of the most beloved in the children's literature of that age.

Even before listening to fairy tales, children feel the need to be told stories or sung to. A love for songs appears especially early due to their rhythm and vivid imagery. The first stories we tell our children only capture their interest when they can relate to them. This is consistent with the child's egocentric nature. Even later on, at least for a while, the story must maintain some connection to the child, allowing the listener to identify with or compare themselves to the hero. This demonstrates child's **subjectivism.**

These early stories were intended not only to entertain but also to teach, often focusing on everyday events such as eating, sleeping, and playing. In Germany, there is a book, particularly suited to very young children, titled *Struwwelpeter* written by a doctor for his young patients. The book became so popular that Charlotte Bühler referred to the developmental stage before the fairy tale period as 'Struwwelpeterzeit' (the Struwwelpeter era). The book was translated into Serbian as *Janko Raščupanko* and into Croatian as *Stanko Čupavko*, though it never achieved the same popularity here as it did in its homeland. It was published in English as *Slovenly Peter* or *Shock-headed Peter*.

The transition from the pre-fairy-tale period to fairy tales is gradual. The first fairy tales a child is introduced to are usually *Little Red Riding Hood*, *The Wolf and the Seven Little Kids*, *Snow White*, and *Hansel and Gretel*. The transition is significant for a child's developmental progress, as it marks a shift from a self-centered perspective to an awareness of others—characters the child has never met and who do not exist within his immediate environment. *Little Red Riding Hood* and even *The Wolf and the Seven Little Kids*, which are often introduced first, share many similarities with the kinds of stories mothers create about obedient or disobedient children. They still maintain a simple plot and lack elements such as transformations of objects or characters.

The fairy tale combines the ordinary with the extraordinary. The fusion of the real and the fantastical is also reflected in its characters. The protagonists are usually children—either from royal families or very poor households—as well as animals or supernatural beings such as fairies, witches, and other magical figures. In addition to these main characters, we occasionally encounter kings, queens, peasants, or soldiers, though they typically serve as supporting roles. All characters are portrayed simply, with only a few traits emphasized, such as kindness, beauty or loyalty. This simplicity of characterization matches a child's limited capability to process, integrate, and abstract complex information.

Animals, in comparison to humans, are sometimes given a slight advantage; they may even take on superior roles, such as judges. In true animal fairy tales, animals are not anthropomorphized; rather they appear in humorous plots bearing traits typical of their real-life counterparts.

Also noteworthy are special creatures like giants, dwarves, witches, and others. Interestingly, Grimm's fairy tales do not feature hybrid beings like bird-men or mermaids. There is a reason for this: the child is not yet ready for such combinations of imagination. The supernatural beings of the first kind possess human characteristics only in altered proportions—such as giants or dwarves. Their presence is always significant, as they appear in moments of difficulty and, through their extraordinary abilities, influence the unfolding of events. All fairy tale characters are essentially archetypes and remain unchanged throughout the story. However, supernatural beings are an exception: they can change depending on the characters they interact with. Often they assume the role of judges, rewarding virtue and punishing wrongdoing.

Thus, fairy tales assign human qualities to objects and animals. Here we encounter the phenomena of **anthropomorphism and personification**, which often occur in children's play. The writer attributes this tendency to the child's inclination to think in analogies.

To cite Bühler,[1] "This inclination of the child to think in analogies, to come up with new creations by analogy, accounts for the multiple transmissions, whether they find their final expression in mental imagination or practical action."

This suggests that the analogical function also plays a significant role in interpreting similar phenomena in children's play. By emphasizing the child's affinity for analogy, this perspective traces various aspects of mental development back to a shared cognitive foundation. However, a closer examination of children's play and its connection to fairy tales reveals that this explanation alone does not fully account for the richness of a child's imaginative experience. The particular state of mind that accompanies the child's imitation games or immersion in the content of fairy tales is not sufficiently addressed. It seems more justified to attribute such deep involvement in fairy tales to the illusionism of a child's imagination.

Another distinctive feature of the fairy tale is its limited description of the characters' environment. We learn certain details almost by chance—for instance, about the golden castle, a marble staircase, or gleaming dresses—usually when the story involves heroes from high-ranking, often royal, families. In the case of a well-to-do character, the child builds mental images based on representations that are poorer in content and more one-dimensional than those of adults, but these images are marked by concreteness and vividness.

When the protagonist in the fairy tale comes from a poverty-stricken family, the description is even sparser; we are simply told that the circumstances are very miserable. Yet, these few details are enough for a child to awaken in him a sense of compassion for the character's pain and suffering. Even a little is enough to stir the child's emotions, which are, by their nature, far more intense than those of adults.

Descriptions in fairy tales exist only where there is a transition from one setting to another. It is interesting that the fairy tale does not recognize social or cultural distinctions. A wretch abandoned in the forest one day may become a queen the next; a peasant's son becomes a king. The world is wide open—everything is possible, says the fairy tale. To the child who has yet to grasp social hierarchies or the limitations imposed by real life, the wonders promised by the fairy tale are not only expected but entirely believable—or, at least, there is no reason to doubt them.

Stern observes that, as in imitation games, the roles of royalty and supernatural beings in fairy tales represent the realization of a child's wishes. Powerless and dependent, the child projects himself into a world of strength, power, and beauty, with the heroes of the tale becoming embodiment of the child himself. In one way or another, the essential thing is that the magical dream described in the fairy tale does not seem strange or impossible to the child, but instead feels familiar and entirely plausible.

---

1 Charlotte Bühler: *Das Märchen und die Phantasie des Kindes*, 1929, p. 25.

Descriptions within the story expand when the action shifts. As the story develops, more details are provided. When possible, these developments unfold as a series of scenes which are depicted primarily through actions.

The fairy tale does not specify in detail the time or place in which its events occur, nor does it offer elaborate descriptions of the objects mentioned. This, once again, corresponds to the nature of the child, allowing the young listener to place the fairy tale within the temporal and spatial framework familiar to him. The essence of a fairy tale does not lie in the description of people, environment, setting, or time, but in the plot that unfolds before the child's eyes.

At this stage of life, children are eager to observe and experience the world; in fairy tales they find nourishment for their visual imagination, and delight in moving from one vivid scene to another. The action unfolding before them holds the greatest appeal, not only because children are naturally active, but also because the energy and movement are at the heart of the fairy tale.

The plot is central. It follows a distinct rhythm consisting of a series of unusual incidents, thrilling events, and various acts and adventures. These elements are bound together by the fairy tale's hero, whom the child loves precisely for the experiences he undergoes and actions he performs.

Miracles also play an important role. Suddenly, the abandoned and the unfortunate receive help, and their circumstances change dramatically. Transformations, miraculous assistance, and similar elements are some of the most crucial components of a fairy tale.

Often the action is driven by strong emotions such as envy or anger, while the desire for adventure and curiosity appear as motivating forces. In general, the fairy tale heroes act out of affect and instinct or under the influence of some authority. They are often young people, but in their overall immature behavior they are children. The moral grounds of some fairy tales are not too high either. Reward and punishment follow directly from the deed. Usually good is rewarded, and evil is punished. But it seems that this justice applies more to the main heroes of the fairy tale who are dear to the child.

When, for example, in *Puss in Boots*, the Wizard suffers even though he was not guilty, all the children follow his suffering with a smile on their faces; their sense of justice does not protest. The actions of the heroes of the fairy tale, just like in the children's lives, move between prohibitions, warnings, and orders.

This tangle of extraordinary and the everyday, presented so simply, resonates deeply with children. Miracles and transformations in a fairy tale do not need to seem impossible to the young mind, and later, as the child matures, he continues to find joy in this play of imagination. The heroes of fairy tales often act without explanation or clear purpose, just as a child does. He does not find their actions strange or impossible, because in many ways, they are children themselves, just like him.

The children's interest is focused mainly on the plot. The way the fairy tale presents the plot seems specially attuned to the child's curiosity and the level of development. The fairy tale makes use of various forms of repetitions—for example, when different characters solve the same task or meet the same fate. This is not only engaging but also serves as a stylistic device. There is usually a structural element that, in the form of a prophecy, admonition, or command, indicates what should be done in a given situation, thereby pointing in the direction of the plot. The exposition then takes up these details, enriches them, and makes them more concrete. Thus stylized, they help the child grasp the fairy tale as a coherent whole.

A fairy tale unfolds its plot step by step, without directly revealing the thought that initiated it—though it describes that thought in detail through events and imagery. Emotional states are often expressed through simple actions that embody them, such as sadness being shown by crying. In this way the fairy tale consistently points outward to the external world, mirroring the child's consciousness, which is similarly directed outward and still distant from an awareness of its own inner life.

Another defining feature of the fairy tale—and of the child's attitude towards the outcome of events—is the desire for a happy ending. The child wants all those events that excited or saddened him to resolve positively, for the hero to emerge victorious. The child feels that his hero deserves sympathy and that the justice demands he wins. The idea that noble ideals could triumph while their bearer is defeated is something a child cannot grasp. For him, the victory of good is embodied in the victory of the hero. Moreover, when we consider that a child feels far more emotionally connected to fairy tale heroes than an adult does to characters in various literary genres, this becomes even clearer. Because of their strong emotions and their immediate identification with characters who feel close to them in every way, the child experiences these figures as being alive. His fear of a tragic ending for the hero, therefore, becomes all the more understandable.

Thus, stringing together episode by episode around its hero, the fairy tale flows vividly before the eyes of the child. It rarely uses metaphors or comparisons. The most common metaphorical transfer that we encounter in a fairy tale is the word 'golden.' Everything can be golden in a fairy tale. This transference of a quality from one object to another where it does not literally belong is a hallmark of the combinative imagination. Groos points to this trait, as we have already seen in the first chapter, when discussing the imaginative tendencies in children. Closely connected to children's inclination to exaggeration, are the techniques of magnification or diminution, which fairy tales also employ. The hero often has to solve several tasks that are increasingly difficult, and objects in fairy tales frequently take on enormous dimensions, if we compare them with such objects in reality. Children delight in these exaggerations, not only because they please their imaginative nature, but also because at this stage of life they are discovering the concept of proportion and the idea fascinates them.

In-depth psychological analysis of fairy tales has revealed the source of children's love for them. It has also shown that **children need fairy tales**. The very fact that they love them so much and constantly ask for them, is a sign that this need is very deep indeed. And yet, I encounter pedagogues who oppose fairy tales. They argue that by transporting children into a world of miracles and fantastical events, fairy tales cause harm. According to them, the deceptive content of fairy tales alienate children from reality.

Depriving a child of fairy tales would indicate a lack of understanding of the nature of his inner life. As long as that strong illusionism persists, the child will seek to satisfy it. Just as he dislikes physical inactivity, he dislikes having an idle imagination. The nature of the fairy tale aligns perfectly with the qualities of his imaginative world. It allows him to visualize the events with which his inner eye keeps his imagination engaged.

While the child is still gradually coming to understand the reality around him, he continues to hold on to his own imagined world, and the fairy tale seems neither strange nor unbelievable. Just as it would not occur to a child to ask where and when such-and-such king or fairy lived, he will not question whether the action of the story could even be possible. Nor, having grown beyond that stage of life, will he accuse us of being liars or deceivers for having sweetened his early years with those beautiful products of imagination.

The attitude a child adopts towards his different roles in play is also reflected in his relationship with fairy tales. If he plays the role of a king and, while immersed in it, behaves as he imagines a king would, he will return to being little Johnny as soon as the game ends. Let's not try to "open the child's eyes" during play by pointing out the unreality of his role! Such an attempt would cause him deep emotional pain. If we frequently engage in this kind of 'enlightenment,' the child will continue to play different roles, but in secret. He will retreat into his own inner world earlier than most, because the force that compels him to play is stronger than we are. Equally strong is his tendency to employ his imagination to sustain this sense of illusion.

We have seen that the illusionistic quality of the imagination naturally fades as development progresses. Not even fairy tales can prevent this. Even if we wanted to, we do not have the means to change the path proscribed by nature. A child's attitude toward fairy tales, once a substantial part of his inner world, changes over time, just as his relationship to play does. Eventually, he will come to understand that the magical world that once made him happy or sad does not actually exist, but he will continue to love it just as deeply as he did before reality set in.

To fear the influence of fairy tales is only justified in case of children who are overly prone to fantasizing or naturally highly excitable. In such instances, a child may indeed linger in the fairy tale world longer than is typical, but such cases are rare. Even though fairy tales can occasionally have a negative impact, they should not be dismissed altogether. Like any other educational tool, they must be used with sensitivity to the individual child's needs and adapted to the specific situation. This is the primary task of a good teacher: to determine which tools are appropriate, and to what extent, in each unique case.

Grimm's fairy tales are often the first stories read to preschool children. Although they mostly correspond to children's nature, some include details that excite or disturb children more than they should. Young children, in particular, are especially highly sensitive to the suffering and struggles of their peers, not only in real life, but also in the world of fairy tales. Occasionally, adults share stories about such intense reactions, either from their own childhood memories, or from experiences with their own children. According to some parents I know, their children cried bitterly upon hearing how the parents in *Hansel and Gretel* wanted to abandon their own children. The idea that parents would deliberately leave their children alone and vulnerable in the forest—a place that itself symbolizes the unknown and frightening—deeply upset and distressed them. The detailed descriptions of merciless tortures and cruel punishments at the end of some fairy tales can also frighten and overwhelm young listeners. Arousing such intense feelings and distress should be avoided. Here nothing remains but to change such details in the course of telling the story.

In some fairy tales, laziness, trickery, or deceit seem to triumph. Certain critics (such as Katz) argue that this is not without consequence for a child's development and may exert a harmful influence. Fairy tales in which virtues such as brotherly love, patience, and kindness are ultimately rewarded, are certainly more advisable. In addition to captivating the child's imagination, they will also touch the soul through the beauty of moral behavior. However, in my view, even those fairy tales which deviate from this moral structure do not have a detrimental effect on children. A child is not introduced to good or evil solely through fairy tales. Real-life experiences, the examples the child observes in his environment, and his natural disposition play a far greater role than the occasional portrayal of negative traits in a story. After all, even in the adult world, such qualities can sometimes lead to success—fairy tales merely reflect this complexity.

I have presented the most important ideas from the psychological analysis of the fairy tale, without strictly adhering to the existing works on the subject, and have, at times, enriched them with my own observations. As we have seen, the fairy tale—in its overall structure—is remarkably attuned to the child's imagination, the characteristics of which were examined in the previous chapters.

The Stories Children Invent

Children do not want to be listeners only; they also want to invent their own stories or narrate experiences while playing with blocks or dolls; they want to entertain their mothers or weave monologues before falling asleep. In the beginning—typical of children—the details from the stories they hear and their own experiences blend in the narration; they also make an effort to invent a story independently.

> Little Ljerka (2 years, 11 months) whose father makes up stories to entertain her, adds her own details.
> Father: "In the park, on the path, there was Momica (their dog)."
> Ljerka: "And a frog."
> Father: "Momica wanted to eat the frog."
> Ljerka: "The frog begged her not to eat him. Then the little girl came (referring to herself) and took them both home."

Although this is not quite a spontaneous product, it is still largely her own. The father provided only the initial stimulus for her imagination. Very prominent here is the self-centeredness of this young child, who relates everything back to herself.

When children begin with the intention of telling a story, they are also able to speak in the third person without involving themselves directly. The example cited in the first chapter, involving three-year-old Hilda, shows that the desire to invent stories about beings unrelated to the child's immediate experience can emerge quite early. These invented stories already display features we have encountered before, such as the flow of the narrative and the way these elements are connected. The course of the story is often determined by an object that catches the eye, a word, or something similar. As a result, storytelling becomes a series of scenes, sometimes organized around the name of a person or thing.

To illustrate how a child progresses in this regard, I will quote part of a story by Stern's son Günter, who was 5 years and 5 months old at the time. The story was inspired by firemen he had seen practicing the day before.

> "And then they fell on a rose tree; it had no thorns, but they still got pricked. Then they plucked them (the roses) and went home to their wives. The firemen were there. Then one fireman made a wreath of light and dark roses for his wife. She was sleeping. The fireman left her the roses softly so she wouldn't wake up. Then the firemen took their large ladder and that's how they climbed up. (Now the picture changes. Among other events, they put out a fire, put the ladder back, and lay down to sleep.) Even the thieves came; they lit up the lamp, but they didn't steal anything."

We can see that the maneuverability of the imagination diminishes here, as the story consists of several smaller parts that separately form wholes. The connection between them is made by the adverb 'then' which serves as a conjunction. The child is already using stylistic devices: dark and light roses, roses without thorns that still sting. Stern interprets this as the child's attempt to introduce something unusual and strange into the story, much like fairy tales do for their listeners.

This example has similarities with that of Velibor, who is a year older. Even though the impetus for the story comes from outside, he spins it further and forgets the task, causing the story to take on the characteristics of spontaneous inventions, or **fabulations**, as Stern calls them. This story is more fully developed in that it brings the events to completion. In some parts, there is a noticeable striving for a fairy tale effect, such as the moment when the entire room shines with gold.

Even a small child is capable of 'building castles in the air,' although to a lesser extent. He also fantasizes about his future. According to Stern's observations, this occurs at the age of five or six. Since a young child still lives entirely in the present, such dreams tend to focus on the near future and are tied to some joyful, anticipated events—for example, a birthday, the celebration of Vrbica holiday (see Notes), or other cherished childhood occasions.

Unlike an adult, a child believes that anything is achievable; he immerses himself in the imaginary as if it were a reality. The poor girl, who was sad that she couldn't wear a new and wonderful dress like her friends for a particular holiday, was comforted by her mother's promise that she would have one soon. The little girl immediately began talking about what color the dress would be and what she would do when she got it— so vividly and in such detail, as if she already had it. Her initial sadness vanished completely. For a child, the illusions of dreams about the future can be so powerful that he lives within them and experiences them to some extent as reality.

Stern distinguishes between **confabulations** related to a child's present and those related to the past. When a child's invention concerns the present, it is considered simply play. A confabulation that connects the child with his past is especially interesting because of its potential outcome. It speaks about something that happened in the past, but it may often resemble a lie or a distortion of memory. It is neither—it is still a play. The child plays with his representations, and connects them with his past, which becomes the center around which imaginary actions unfold.

We were talking about Hilda's sewing box. Eva (3 years, 5 months) said during the game:
"Grandma gave me a box too."
Hilda and Günter were very surprised. I explained:
"Ah, Eva is just joking," to which she replied:
"No, she really gave it to me."

Since the older children were present, the mother couldn't let the childish game continue and asked Eva to bring the box. Eva became upset and almost cried; it took quite a while before she finally admitted—after being repeatedly asked—that she didn't have a box. The child had persistently claimed she had one, driven by her desire to preserve the illusion of reality.

Fictitious stories of this kind, in which the child talks about his past—much like his stories about other people or toys—can be considered a part of his creative efforts. What justifies setting them apart is the fact that, to those unaware that a child turns anything into play and that he enjoys playing with words and events, such inventions may appear as lies. That is why one must be very cautious when judging the actions and words of a small child.

In his eyes, things do not have to be as they appear to adults. He has his own childish perspective on everything. Disturbing his illusions throws him into a bad mood and often brings him to tears. This does not mean that he should be left without educational guidance in this regard, but the educator should employ utmost tact. Only when the child becomes more developed and capable of better understanding of our expectations, can we help him learn to distinguish situations in which he can let his imagination run wild, from those in which he must adhere to reality. Often, when a child tries to explain something to himself or to others, or to recount how something happened, he creates romanticized stories in which his imagination works freely— sometimes to the point of resembling a lie.

> I noticed that Mara (3 years, 6 months) was no longer playing with her doll. When I asked her where the doll was, she said:
> "The doll fell from the chimney, so I took her to the hospital." When I asked how the doll got there, she replied:
> "I put up a ladder and cleaned the chimney. The doll came to help, but she fell."

This sounds like a lie, just like the story about the sewing box, but it is nothing more than playful storytelling given a special twist by the broken doll. My question served as the incentive for the story to develop in that direction. Indeed, there was a pipe running through the ceiling of the room that her mother sometimes cleaned. The little girl enjoyed climbing the ladder very much. In her story, she transfers the role of her mother to herself. The doll fictitiously fulfills her wishes—which seemed dangerous to the girl—and she becomes a victim of disobedience.

That an observation can trigger a lively work of imagination, is evidenced by a charming story I cite here according to the German translation of Sully's work:[1]

---

1 James Sully: *Untersuchungen über die Kindheit*, 1897, p. 49.

A little three-year-old boy saw a vagabond approaching and exclaimed:

> "Look at that poor man, mother! He has a sick leg."
>
> Then, guided by a romantic notion he had at the moment, he made up a story: "He mounted a very big horse, and stepped on a very big stone. He hurt his poor leg, so he had to walk with a big stick. We have to heal him."
>
> After thinking for a while, the boy added:
>
> "Mom, go and kiss that place and heal him like you heal me when I am hurt."

One look at the miserable appearance of the tramp was enough for him to concoct this romantic, sentimental little story.

A child's desire to explain or interpret how a phenomenon that interests him came about often leads to inventing stories. Groos's three-year-old nephew, who chose North Berlin as the setting for his stories, once told this:

> "In North Berlin, there are rabbits and puppies on the roof.
>
> They climb some ladders and play… and then... and then there is the phone, you know, a long rope, so they go to Stuttgart on it. That's why they are now with us."

Groos cited this little story because the child used it in order to explain a phenomenon that interested him, in a way similar to the function of a myth. Groos drew a parallel between this story and the myths of primitive peoples, and found that both tend to explain an occurrence by inventing an event from which they then derive the whole phenomenon.

> "Long ago," an Australian tells his children, "this black-and-white bird was completely black. Then it got involved in a war and began painting itself white. But when it was only halfway done, the enemy arrived, and the bird had to go into battle half white and half black. That's why its descendants have this unusual plumage."

These little stories are prompting me to mention again the opinion of the author of *Fairy Tale and Child's Imagination*, Charlotte Bühler. She denies almost all combinative ability in a child's imagination. But what else is the story of the three-year-old boy in Sully's example, if not a new creation of his imagination? It may not be a composition rich in detail and as complex as one given by a writer, but it is fully adapted to the current needs of the little storyteller. The child's naïveté and his indifference to the relationship between his creation and reality give it a special freshness and originality that reveals the creative imagination of a young child.

When analyzing the stories in which the child himself plays the main role versus those in which he mostly tries to explain something, I noticed a difference. The latter creations form wholes. All the examples mentioned here come from children no older than four—an age when, in the first type of fables, the narrative still jumps from scene to scene, and the imagination remains highly fluid.

When a child inserts his 'self' into an invented story and makes it the focal point of the events described, this integration can be understood as the result of relating the event to his own experience. In doing so, the child perceives these imagined actions—at least partially—as real, connecting them to himself as he does in play.

But how do things stand in the stories in which the child creates to explain something? All stories in this category are short. I think the reason for this is that they have a different starting point. Here, the child wants to explain something to himself or to others, sets a specific goal, and organizes everything around it. The key difference between the two types of storytelling lies in their underlying motivation and in the attitude the child adopts toward each.

In the first case, the child gives himself over to the flow of the performance, intending to have fun and use his imagination in the best way he knows how. As he develops and learns to focus on larger wholes—a process tied to the growth of attention and will—he becomes better at connecting his stories and even develops modest stylistic ambitions (for example, using expressions like "light and dark roses"), in pursuit of certain effects.

In the second case, he uses his most developed creative force—his imagination—to solve the problem he has set for himself. In this case, the story must be well connected, because it pursues a specific goal.

To determine whether these observations are correct, it would be necessary to collect and compare more material. So far, no one has pointed out this phenomenon, but the material currently available to me supports it.

Child's Play

Playing and childhood belong to each other. We can also imagine older children playing—those beyond the age studied in this work—or even the playing of adults, because they have their own games. But we cannot imagine a young child without play, because playing is his whole world. A young child lives and works in that world, unless difficult circumstances force him to leave it too early. A school-aged child already divides his energies between work and play, while for an adult playing is a leisure activity and a break from the monotony of life.

We have seen how deeply a child's imagination permeates the reality around him. It is natural for him to incorporate it into his games. In fact, playing is an area in which the imagination will manifest itself most vividly. So far we have discussed the qualities of a child's imagination. Now we will focus more on his play to determine its significance for childhood and the role that imagination has in it.

When we observe the joy and delight of a child at play, when we see how he dedicates himself to it with his whole soul, and how challenging even the small mishaps can be, we begin to understand what play must mean to a child—how important it truly is. But what, in essence, is play? And why does a child play? First, let us compare an adult and a child in their most frequent daily activities: an adult at work and a small child at play.

While playing, the child is working. An adult works by performing tasks. Both are essentially engaged in activity, but the nature of this activity is accompanied by a different state of consciousness.

A man who is working strives to achieve something; he has a specific task in mind. His work is entirely directed toward that task, serving its realization. There is a goal, and his work is the means to achieve it. The goal arises out of some human need, whether spiritual or physical. The work leaves traces in the form of a tangible product or accomplishment that serves this goal. Working toward it can be difficult and it is often accompanied by discomfort. Yet he perseveres, driven by a need that compels him to go forward.

When a child plays, he also creates something, whether it is real like shaping a pile of sand, or imagined, like picking invisible apples. However, for the child, the product of his creativity is not the main focus; the primary focus is the activity itself. If a child is building a house from blocks and suddenly thinks of something else, he will tear down the house without regret. The act of creating is what matters most. Most of the time, if the play becomes unpleasant or another game offers greater joy, the child will simply abandon the first game and start a new one. A child plays for the sake of playing. That would be my answer to the question of what play really is.

Groos, Stern and other childhood psychologists confirm these findings, as they contrast play with work and identify what is important in one activity and what is important in another. Unlike with adults at work, it is not always possible to see the specific need that drives a child to action. However, experience shows that a child plays best when he determines the type and duration of the game himself. When the game loses its appeal, he stops playing. He plays for the pleasure that play provides him. Thus, play is a spontaneous activity of the highest order.

When observed from the outside, play may appear to be a free and aimless activity, especially when compared to work, which is typically directed toward fulfilling external tasks. However, in its essence, play is far from aimless. A healthy child becomes so deeply absorbed in play that it is evident this intensity arises from within—a powerful inner drive, an irresistible need.

What seems like freedom from an external viewpoint is, in reality, an expression of inner necessity—a manifestation of instinct. Thus, although play may appear voluntary and spontaneous, it is, at its core, governed by a compelling internal force that the child himself is not consciously aware of. Play is not merely a result of one of the many instincts, as William Stern rightly observed, but rather a unique form of activity through which all instincts are expressed.

Spencer ascribes a reason why the children play to the accumulation of energy in the nervous system. According to him, children are not drained by life's struggles and demands, so they have an excess of strength. This accumulated energy provides a physiological stimulus for physical activity. "When this force, which longs to be released, does not find external cause for activity, the body creates one by stimulating the activity through play.[1]

Certainly, the condition for play is a healthy and strong body, but, first of all, playing is not always a game of stimulation, and the only cause for playing cannot be to get rid of the accumulated energy, because a "small child plays in the morning, evening, and night, as long as he has the strength." (Ibid. p. 77) I believe, that the excess of energy alone can not explain the essence of play. We need to delve deeper into the subject.

Inasmuch as the living being that is better prepared for life at the beginning has less need and opportunity for development, the degree of his preparedness determines both the scope and the manner in which he will live. Higher animals have a long childhood. Human childhood is the longest, but a child is also the most feeble and weakest at the beginning of life, because he is the least completed. As Groos points out, "A very young child is powerless to learn to help himself." In this early stage, the child's overwhelming need to play is not directed by specific goals but by an inherent urge simply to "be doing something." This tendency is a defining characteristic of childhood.

Based on this aspect of human nature, childhood serves as a critical period for the development of both spiritual and physical strength, preparing the child for later life in an environment that requires almost constant coping. Groos famously stated: "We do not play because we are children, but we are children because we play." His theory of play—what he calls the theory of **self-education** or **training**—captures the essential role of play in early human development. His perspective offers the most coherent explanation for the phenomena associated with play during the formative years of life.

There are other theories that seek to explain the reasons behind playing. I will briefly mention only those that are most relevant to early childhood. American psychologist Harvey E. Carr believes that the value of many games lies in their ability to provide an outlet for certain preserved instincts which, if expressed in everyday life, might be more harmful than beneficial. Play, in his view, offers a safe space for the revival and expression of these instincts. This "**theory of catharsis**" (or purification) can be extended even further—it does not necessarily have to refer to the awakening of instincts alone.

---

1 X. Spencer's quote as cited by Karl Groos in *Das Seelenleben des Kindes*, 1921 p. 60.

Édouard Claparéde states that Carr's idea cited by Groos "does not refer to suppression, but only to the redirection of harmful tendencies.[1]

We can retain the assumption of actual catharsis if we allow that it is the emotions, rather than specific activities, that are being vented, and that this release is only momentary, not permanent. For instance, when a child gets into a fight with a peer, he does not completely lose his fighting instinct—an impulse which may be vital in more serious situations. Rather, at that moment he momentarily releases the emotion associated with that instinct. Without this outlet, the same emotional buildup could otherwise lead to socially harmful behavior, even in the absence of a real provocation. Understood in this way, the theory of catharsis complements Groos's theory. While Groos emphasizes the development of tendencies needed for future life, catharsis focuses on the present—allowing unwanted or excessive emotions to be released through play in a constructive and socially acceptable way.

Expounding on the theories of play, Stern emphasizes its significance for the present moment, pointing out how the aspirations that shape the child's current world are reflected in play. Certain relationships become quite evident here: The urge to explore, play, embellish, create, and imitate directly lead to specific forms of play. Indeed, all of these drives exist in the child, who longs to satisfy them.

But didn't we claim at the beginning of this chapter that play is the way in which instincts manifest at this age? Through play, the child seeks to fulfill his basic need for activity, which is why play always serves his present experience. When the drive for knowledge arises, he pursues it because of this innate urge, which directly impacts his present. However, the true significance of such instincts lies in their role in shaping the future, much like play rehearses life to come.

Psychoanalysis suggests that the sexual drive dominates the child to a large extent, but the child can vent it only in play, in a symbolic way.

According to **individual psychology**, the drive for power serves to achieve protection from the feelings of weakness. In other words, a child's dependence on adults and any perceived deficiencies in spiritual or physical abilities can give rise to feelings of inferiority and helplessness. Play provides a sense of satisfaction by offering a fictitious feeling of power and dominance.

Stern and other psychologists criticize psychoanalysis for portraying the child as a wholly sexual being—and they are probably right. If such a drive exists in a young child, it must manifest itself only in a vague and indistinct form. It is difficult to imagine that, in this particular regard, a small child could closely resemble an adult, especially when we know that, in other areas, his

---

1 Karl Groos: *Das Seelenleben des Kindes,* 1921, p. 74.

mental life exhibits distinctly different characteristics. If we were to assume that this theory is correct, then it could, to some extent, be interpreted through the lens of the concept of purification, as expanded by Edouard Claparède. In that case, the emotions accompanying this drive would find their expression and resolution in play.

The view held by individual psychology that play acts as a **protection**—an unconscious defense against life which presses on the child emphasizing its weakness—can be justified in many ways. While constantly submitting to reality, the child finds satisfaction in becoming the master of the game, finding relief from feelings of weakness by playing the role of someone powerful and strong. Indeed, if we understand the meaning of playing in this light, it primarily serves the child's present situation. But that alone does not sufficiently explain why the child plays. Only when this perspective is linked to the theory of **self-education** does it provide a comprehensive understanding of the purpose of playing.

According to the **individual psychology**, the way a child reacts in play allows us to observe, quite early on, the individual traits of the future adult. Thus, play is given significance not only for the present but also for the future. In short, it could be said that play truly serves the development of all the forces present in child—therefore, it serves the child's future—while also holding meaning for the present, as it is a form through which the child can express various feelings associated with instinctual drives, as well as emotions that arise from contact with the external world. In the light of this, the theories of Groos, Carr and Spencer seem to provide sufficient explanation of the importance of play in early childhood.

It is precisely this dual role of play—serving both the present and the future— that stands out most clearly. All the basic abilities given to humans must first be practiced through play. Before they truly become part of the child's repertoire, sitting, walking, and speaking all pass through a playful stage. Thought, imagination, and the whole spiritual life of a human being are first encountered in play. Through it, the child begins to be shaped as a member of society, learning to obey rules and to subordinate personal will to the collective order. While the child is still weak and dependent on adults for everything, unable to meet his own needs, he willingly exposes himself to great challenges in play, confronts obstacles, overcomes them, or occasionally succumbs. In doing so, the child becomes the master of his own body and learns how to control situations in life.

The basis for all this, as we have seen, lies in his strong desire for activity—a force that permeates the entire childhood. Human instincts and functions, rooted in this drive, are activated and shaped in play.

Thus, despite his real weakness and need for help and protection, the child possesses a world of his own in which he is strong and powerful—a world where he can act freely precisely because he uses tools and means he can manage without fear of consequences. The setbacks he encounters may, at worst, teach him something and add to his experience, but will not expose him to real danger. A stick or a chair, used as a substitute for a horse, is sufficient for his imaginative play and, at the same time, spares him the difficulties he would face with a real horse which lie far beyond his current abilities.

The form of play depends on the child's stage of development. As the child progresses through different phases, the nature of play evolves, shaped by emerging drives. He must first learn to control his organs and limbs, then develop his mental and emotional faculties. Once he achieves a degree of self-mastery, the child must begin to prepare for his future social role.

Accordingly, play can be categorized into two types: individual play which promotes personal development, and social play, which prepares the child for functioning within a community. In the following section, we will primarily focus on Stern's *Psychology of Early Childhood* (*Psychologie der Frühen Kindheit*).

Individual Games

Play primarily serves to develop the body, and the child's earliest games are related to this purpose. These include an infant's cooing, early limb movements, attempts to sit up, crawl, grasp objects, bang them, and so on. Even later, when the child has learned to sit and walk, the urge for movement fills most of his time: The child runs, jumps, chases, climbs, and practices balance by walking along the edge of a path or on a narrow board. These lively body movements are often accompanied by shouting, exclamations, and singing. When several children join in, the running, shouting, and jumping can evoke in an adult the image of wild people dancing around a fire—so great can be the energy and unrestrained liveliness in their play.

These games primarily meet the child's need for movement. When a small child plays in the sand, he is not yet 'building' anything nor has he set a specific goal. This movement for the sake of movement helps him exercise his limbs and develop motor control. For that reason, neither the shape nor the function of a toy matters. He throws it, lifts it, shakes it, regardless of whether the toy can serve any particular or defined purpose in the game.

This natural urge to move is accompanied by an urge to imitate. Children mimic walking like soldiers, horse's trot, and so on. In jumping and running as in all skills through which a child gradually masters his body, there appears a strong element of competition. A desire to prove one's skill and assert self-worth is already beginning to take shape. These games lie at the heart of childhood.

At first, the child does not change the shape of objects, but interacts with them by hitting them, making sounds, raising and lowering the lids of the containers, or throwing them. Any object can serve equally well as a toy. In this respect a piece of wood or a rag has the same value, but the child soon begins to change the shape of objects.

Following the early games mentioned above, another group of games emerges in which the child strives to master objects. This happens quite early: Stern has labeled these as **destructive games**; they are of the type quite easily noticed by anyone observing children's activities. A toy that appeals to an adult, as well as a piece of old paper, can equally fall victim to this childish need for destruction.

Stern finds that the cause of these immature actions lies, in most cases, in the child's desire to test his strength on objects. By overcoming their resistance, he destroys them, experiencing the feeling of being the cause of something happening. Nowhere can this awareness be more strongly manifested than in demolition, because it requires neither deliberation nor perseverance. Perhaps this form of play can be primarily understood as an unconscious expression of child's strength and a pursuit of power, especially in the earlier phase of development.

However, in many cases, the cause of the destruction may also be the pursuit of knowledge. By the third or fourth year, the desire to find out what is inside a toy plays a role in the child's disassembling or breaking it. In my presence, a three-year-old who was smashing a tin soldier volunteered the information that he was doing it because he wanted to see what was inside. It is therefore quite likely that the pleasure the child finds in the manifestation of his strength is accompanied quite early on by his desire to understand how things work.

At a higher level of play, we find **constructive** games: These require perseverance in achieving a goal, which indicates that the child is capable of synthesis. Such games already exhibit the child's creative tendencies. The ability to construct also appears quite early, as demonstrated in arranging nuts, stones, and other objects that the child uses with the intention of building a train or representing another new object.

These two types of games—destructive and constructive—appear almost side by side. Though different in terms of outcomes, they are partly similar in aspirations from which they arise. In the first type, the child feels joy in being the cause of something important to him, in the second type, when an intention to do something already exists, the child feels happy that he is actually able to construct something by himself.

As development progresses, constructive games begin to dominate. These games include building with blocks or other suitable material, drawing, shaping objects from sand, dough or other malleable substances, and crafting items such as paper or flower wreaths. I observed children in the nursery school while they were engaged in such activities. They worked without adult supervision at that moment, therefore their combinations were completely free. The boys, in particular, constructed representations of airplanes using cardboard. Many children showed a sense of harmony in color matching—they produced tastefully composed drawings, flowers, and other objects. The individual differences caught my eye: Certain children knew what they wanted and worked towards their goals; others were not aware of the nature of their creations.

Generally speaking, among children of approximately the same age as the ones present in this class, these differences do not only reflect the greater or lesser ability of their imagination, but also the degree of their general development. It would be worthwhile to connect the creative results of these children's activities to their success in reproducing stories and other types of imaginative work. Although I did not study this relationship in depth, I did notice a significant overlap in individual accomplishments. The children who were able to reproduce the fairy tales they heard fairly well were also the ones who could better describe the pictures they saw. When asked what a particular shape represented, they did not say, "I don't know what it is," but they readily explained the meaning of individual designs on paper, saying, for example, that they had drawn people in an airplane or something similar.

Stern finds that these constructive games are particularly indicative of the difference between the sexes, both in terms of time frame and the form in which they appear. He identifies this difference as early as the second year of a child's life. According to him, boys at that age already engage in constructive play by arranging objects. By the age of four to six, the need for construction becomes so strong that they surpass many girls in this activity. Although girls also develop interest in constructive games, boys consistently remain ahead of them in this area.

Stern also notices a difference in regard to imitation. Many of these games are played according to established models, to which the child adheres to varying degrees—or not at all—sometimes choosing instead to imitate objects he has already seen. While playing, the child may invent freely, as when he creates a new pattern from scraps of cardboard or other stackable materials, or he builds a new structure according to his imagination. Imitation is more pronounced in girls' games than in boys'. Boys tend to construct based on their own observations or spontaneous combinations, while girls are generally satisfied with imitating a model.

It would be of great interest to see how the children are influenced by the **role of sexes** they observe in their daily lives, and how these influences might reflect their preferences for different types of play, but that would warrant a further, rather extensive study.

Stern gathered the data for these claims by observing his own children, and also drew upon the Skupins' diary about their child. It is likely he also relied on broader experiences observing the imaginative play of children in general. His conclusions in this respect correspond quite well with the facts, but a more comprehensive study of this aspect of children's games would not be superfluous, because a larger body of evidence would make it easier to separate general from individual. This would also make it easier to determine what truly characterizes the play of children of one gender, and to distinguish it from the individual characteristics of a particular child's play, since, when observations are limited to a small number of cases, it it is easy to mistake an individual child's traits for universal features of childhood.

The child devotes a lot of his time to **games of impersonation**. In them, the impulse to imitate is expressed more directly than in previously mentioned activities. Groos called them **"games of illusion."** As we have already noted, illusionism is an important feature of imagination in early childhood. It plays a major role in imitation games, where the child assigns to himself various roles, reenacting events he has already experienced, as these mirror the life around him.

Just as a child assigns different roles to himself, he also assigns them to the objects he needs in that game. In doing so, we again encounter that characteristic of a child's imagination, which we called indifference to the external form of the object used in play. A chair can become a train; a stick, a horse that is patted or beaten because it "won't go." Here, on one hand, we refer to his endowing of external form to an object that does not have it; on the other hand, attributing to it the mental qualities. Objects come to life and take on human characteristics, as shown in the following vignette.

Little Ljerka (3 years old) returned home after being away for six weeks and ran straight to the room where her toys were kept. The reunion was very cordial. She spoke to each toy and asked her doll: "How are you, my little dolly?" She then inquired whether the doll was ill and said that she was going to smear its sick leg with iodine, just as her father does for her. She patted the ball and talked to it. The reunion lasted nearly two hours, during which she spoke to each of her toys. This is what she said to the stone that fell out of her hand: "You're restless, you won't listen. I'll beat you up."

But sometimes a child doesn't even need toys to play with—perhaps the vividness of a child's imagination is most accentuated in the games in which there are no objects and yet the game flows as vividly as if the child sees and really lives the scenes being represented.

Mara (3 years, 6 months) brings her sick 'little girls' to her father. He has to rock them in his arms while she runs to the doctor. The doctor gives her the medication which she then uses to rub on the girls. All the while, she runs back and forth between her father and the ottoman, all in motion, animated—as if these invisible little girls are in mortal danger and she must save them. When I ask where the girls are, she convincingly points to a spot on her father's arm, then immediately dashes off to rescue another one.

In another episode, Mara's little fist represents a train moving across the table—sometimes faster, sometimes slower. I am told to get on the train, which means placing my hand on hers. Suddenly, Grandma Naka appears in the game—an association, as Mara travels to her grandmother by train.

> Mara: "The train disappears. Grandma Naka brings out dinner, but only for me. I give her some food; she chews on it."

Nothing tangible was necessary for this game, other than movement and narrative; everything else was compensated by her imagination. In such games, movement is the main thing. She performed it for herself, fulfilling an inner need to engage in expressive action. The apparent purpose of this activity was entirely shaped by her imagination, and how much freedom her activity had here! Her play was not constrained by the need for real objects; its very impulse was freedom itself. It is telling that such games are lost with children's development. An older child almost always needs some real support for play, while a younger one is content to evoke entire scenes through gestures alone. This shift reflects a broader developmental change: the gradual decline of illusionism in childhood.

A child imitates the life around him by bringing it into his games and taking on various roles. He sells goods, buys old things, plays a merchant, and more. In doing so, he imitates not only the movements of such persons, but also their work and words. This is more than external mimicry; it is a deep immersion in the emotional life of the people he portrays. Just as he once projected his own mental qualities onto objects, he now projects himself into the inner states of others. While playing a role, he expects the world to respond to him in a way that is in harmony with that role.

In these games, the distinctive quality of a child's imagination—what Groos, following K. Lange, calls **conscious self-deception**—reveals itself in full force.

> We have already encountered this trait earlier when discussing illusionism, but these games are the domain in which it reigns supreme. The child's wholeheartedness and devotion to the role are profound, while everything else recedes into the background of consciousness.

Role-playing is especially important for the development of the child's inner life, because by imitating emotions and actions of the model, the child enriches himself with experiences of others, precisely through his transference into their roles. Here, the impulse to imitate and the child's need for activity come together, and—guided by imagination—lend play both beauty and purpose. Seen in this light, the significance of such games provides strong support for the **theory of self-education** through play.

On the other hand, Stern, relying to some extent on Alfred Adler, connects these role-playing games with child's unconscious tendency to compensate for his feelings of weakness by creating a fiction of strength and power. A child who feels weak and dependent, who needs help from others in everything, and who constantly encounters obstacles in his movement and action, may treat a doll or any other toy as an all-powerful master would, thereby unconsciously exacting revenge for the limitations he faces in real life.

"Fiction is therefore nothing but an internal rebellion against the real feeling of inferiority." This is the view of individual psychology regarding these games. Stern expands this explanation and connects it with the **theory of self-education**, according to which the play serves the future. He argues that it indicates the power and success the child anticipates in life. The child wants, he says, to prove to himself and others—or at least to pretend—that he can do something, that he can master a task, and that other people or objects might depend on his help.

Both of these interpretations of role-playing touch on layers of the psyche of which the child is unaware during his play. One perspective highlights the positive side, the other the negative, but both rely on his desire to have a sense of power. Observing children during many such games reveals only that this feeling of power underlies their play; whether a negative or positive tendency prevails, or whether both play a role simultaneously, remains unclear. Thus, when a little girl plays the role of a mother and behaves autocratically toward her little brother, scolding him for every move, one can discern both tendencies in her behavior.

This perspective can indeed help make many children's role-playing more comprehensible. Since we accept that such feelings can be a significant factor in adult life, there is no reason why they should be any less important to the child.

Even through simple observation, one can see that illusionistic games bring change into a life of a child; they expand it and enrich its content. Through such play, the child absorbs many customs, beliefs, and ways of life from his environment, thereby developing close bonds with them from an early age. **"Long before school begins to consciously transmit spiritual benefits to the young generation, the child has already begun to take care of the historical continuity independently,"** says Stern.[1]

Thus, these games cultivate both mental and physical capacities, serving as strong preparation for the child's later role in society. Imitation games may be solitary, but quite early on, children begin to engage in them with peers. We will now turn our attention to the latter as we explore the role of play within the social environment.

Social Games

The child's first teammates are not other children but adults. They accept his games and often initiate them. Beginning around the fourth year, the child

---

1 William Stern: *Psychologie der frühen Kindheit*, 1930, p. 269.

58

starts to develop a strong desire for the company of his peers who offer a greater degree of understanding due to shared interests and similar emotional level of development. This mutual understanding intensifies the play, makes it more lively, and increases the child's enjoyment.

The highest form of play in early childhood, in which the social interaction emerges, is the **joined imitation games**. These naturally require a division of roles, requiring each child to understand and accept their part and to follow the rules of the game. While the child, who at this stage is merely playing a role, can act freely, and can, within the limits of his mood and skill, play that role more or less faithfully, these games still demand a grasp of details and a performance which considers the objective of the game. As such, they require a higher level of overall development. For the game to proceed smoothly, children must possess stronger synthetic ability and a longer power of concentration. These imitation or role-playing games are influenced by the type and quality of the environment in which the children live—the events that take place, the occupations they observe, seasonal work, everyday occurrences, and even occasional events such as the arrival of a circus.

Illusionistic games last throughout childhood, evolving in form to match the child's development and changing interests. Their essence remains constant at both higher and lower levels, regardless of whether they serve a child's individual or social character. Although these games emerge as early as in the second year of life, they not only become more complex during early childhood and bear more and more the character of the whole, but they also become richer in details. A younger child may enact the same role with fewer movements, while an older one elaborates on it, making it appear more realistic. With further development, the child's previous disregard of reality, once fueled by imagination, gradually fades.

The first games in which children play together do not exhibit a high level of interaction, unlike the fully developed social games of imitation. The children may be playing more alongside one another rather than with one another. They merely run, jump, shout together. Such games often become so lively and exuberant that adults may find them difficult to tolerate.

Almost simultaneously, *kolo* (see Notes) and other similar group games begin to emerge, involving larger groups of children engaged in synchronized activity. These games prescribe the manner of performance and require all participants to move in unison, functioning as a cohesive whole. Because these group movements are rhythmic and accompanied by a melody, they hold particular appeal for young children.

The earliest games of this kind are simple, but over time their performance grows increasingly complex. Unlike imitation games, which arise spontaneously from the children who play them, these are passed down from older children to younger ones.

Although to a lesser extent than role-playing games, these games also require a certain level of maturity, as participants must follow rules and remember the sequence of movements. Thus, once the children have sufficiently developed through individual play, they begin training for their future social role through these shared activities. In such social games, content, melody, and physical movement are often combined; they also tend to acquire a dramatic character by imitating actions or events from the lives of children or adults. The fact that a group of children performs these elements in unison, enhances the game's impact on each participant by fostering a sense of shared experience. The child may even begin to sense, although not very clearly, that beauty and greatness often arise from collective effort. The principal educational value of these games lies in preparation for future social work.

Other types of social games, such as fighting games, extend beyond the boundaries of early childhood and will therefore not be explored here. In addition to the review above, which outlines the general characteristics of the types of games that prevail at the preschool level, we should examine more closely how an individual child relates to play—and how play, in turn, relates to childhood as a whole.

Social games require the participation of several children. The liveliness with which they bring their fantasies to life—their energy and inventiveness— varies from child to child. One may contribute more ideas to the same game than another, and the richness of those ideas may also differ. It is only natural, then, that in group play individual character becomes even more pronounced.

Children differ in agility and expressiveness, in their ability to cope with new situations, and in how well they grasp different aspects of the game. These games require a certain degree of organization. Someone must lead. As a result, the quickest or the most skilled child often takes charge. This leader is frequently an older child, though not always. Sometimes, a younger child assumes the role, because he may have a better understanding of how to organize the game and assume the leadership. This is how, through play, the first authority figures emerge within the group of children.

What is imitated—and how the imitation is carried out—depends on the child's development, innate dispositions, interests, and gender. Imitation is not always a strict repetition of an action or situation; as children grow, they move beyond simple mimicry, introducing new details into their games, constructing imaginative scenarios, and combining diverse elements. This is only natural when we consider their general liveliness, their constant need to act, to transform, to give their play as much zest as possible.

"The imitation of adults in play serves as the stimulus and starting point for both the game itself and the process of formation and creation. At the same time, these actions facilitate the transition to self-initiated activity, discovery, invention, and the early manifestation of the beginnings of productive imagination," writes Meumann.[1] This reflects the instinctive

---

1 Ernst Meumann: *Vorlesungen zur Einführung in die experimentelle Pädagogik*, 1916, I Band, p. 529.

basis of play, which serves, as we have seen, to foster the development of all human capacities.

The internal drive that determines what kind of play the child will choose, is crucial, because, as Stern states, "through it, the laws of internal development manifest with such force that children in the most diverse countries and epochs, despite all differences in environmental conditions, develop the same instincts for various types of play at the same age. Thus, games involving the throwing of objects, caring for dolls, or engaging in pretend battles transcend time and space, social strata, national identities, and levels of cultural progress. While the materials children use to express their instincts in games of movement, care, and struggle may change with the surrounding world, the fundamental forms of play remain unaffected."[1]

Every type of play carries an inherent educational element, making play a form of **unintentional self-education**. The question, then, is how and to what extent a teacher can harness a child's spontaneity for educational purposes without depriving the play of its freshness and originality.

The influence of adults should primarily consist of giving the child an opportunity to play as much as he likes. A child needs to play actively and frequently in order to develop properly. If the conditions in which a child grows up force him into any form of labor before the appropriate time, he may be harmed in many ways. Full and comprehensive development in early childhood is possible only through play. A child learns more through play during the early years of life, than at any other stage.

For play to be truly engaging, a child—once mature enough—primarily needs to play in the company of peers. Children connect more easily when they are on the same emotional and developmental level and share similar interests.

Among friends, the child does not necessarily encounter only benevolent and lenient teammates who unconditionally cater to his wishes— as adults often do, sometimes condescendingly, treating a child more like a toy than a person. An older child senses the limitations of such treatment, and seeks other children of similar age or capability, for whom play, like for him, is a serious and absorbing activity—just as important as the work is for an adult, or perhaps even more so.

For the game to flow smoothly while retaining its excitement, a child often needs to compromise, sometimes even giving up a toy, so that another child can use it. He must adhere to the rules, which requires self-discipline, perseverance in completing assigned task, and a willingness to submit to the structure of the game. Through such shared experiences the child begins to learn compassion for the weak and gains a concrete understanding of justice and injustice. At

---

1 William Stern: *Psychologie der Frühen Kindheit*, 1930, p. 270.

this stage of life, group play is one of the most powerful tools for building character.

Preschool education plays a big role in a person's life, as it lays the foundation for future personality. A child who has grown stronger mentally and physically through play and has acquired certain habits needed for everyday life is better prepared for school and more resilient in facing the internal struggles and challenges of puberty and later life.

"Start with the child" is the guiding principle of current pedagogy. If this method of educational influence looks promising, then its value for a preschool child is of particular importance. "The right education coincides for a few years with the right occupation," write David and Rosa Katz in their insightful book on education in preschool age.[1] The key is to ensure that the child engages in meaningful activities that foster independence, and that his interests not only entertain him but also contribute to his development, allowing useful habits to become an integral part of his daily life.

Toys, being the necessary tools, have an important role in playing. If the circumstances in which a child grows up prevent parents from providing tools, the child, when a bit older, will often gather objects like boxes, colored paper, and scraps of fabric, treating them as treasured possessions and keeping them carefully for some time. Certainly, the scarcity of toys has its effect on child's games. He strives for variety by frequently changing games, though the lack of materials can hinder his combinations. It is not advisable to give children too many toys, as an overabundance may lead to a sense of over-saturation and reduce the special fondness children typically have for their toys.

When we say a child needs a toy, it does not mean he needs an expensive or a complicated one—often designed more to impress adults than to meet the needs of a child. A choice of a toy should reflect the child's nature. A toy that he can handle freely, without worrying about damaging it, is dearer to the child than the one that initially delights him with its novelty but soon breaks due to its complexity.

A small car that starts automatically may attract his attention and curiosity for a while, but it will never provide as much incentive for play as a cart—one in which he can put his dolls and animals, take them for a walk, or use in many creative ways. Durability increases a toy's value in the eyes of a child. A doll that a girl can bathe, dress, and rock—one she can play with freely without fear of breaking it and being scolded—is far more enjoyable than a delicate, decorative doll she is barely allowed to touch. The more the toy's design stimulates the child's imagination, the more it is loved.

---

1 David and Rosa Katz: *Die Erziehung im Vorschulpflichtigen Alter*, 1925.

That's exactly why building blocks and similar toys are so popular with children. They serve as valuable play tools throughout this developmental period. A two-year-old can occupy himself by stacking them, arranging them in simple patterns, or experimenting with them in novel ways. A more developed child can use them to create more complex structures, increasing his spatial awareness and early understanding of geometry. These toys often allow a child to play independently for an hour, two hours, or even longer. It is important to teach a child that, when he is done playing, the toys should be put away in their assigned place. This practice helps instill early habits of neatness, order and independence—qualities essential for later life. The habit of tidying up after play should be encouraged across all types of games.

Young children delight in crumpling or tearing paper, while older ones enjoy cutting out various shapes. At first, the child is not guided by a specific goal— he cuts paper because he finds the action enjoyable. When one day, driven by his illusionistic nature, he discovers in a random shape a similarity to an object, he begins cutting paper with intention and purpose. This marks the beginning of more creative work, and the teacher can nurture this creativity by assigning specific tasks.

In this activity we can distinguish the same developmental stages as in drawing. For example, a child might accidentally create a symmetrical shape, and take great delight in it. Children are also particularly drawn to colored paper because of their early sensitivity to color. Given how versatile paper can be for young children, educators should provide plenty of it. To support both safety and independence, they should also provide rounded-tip scissors, allowing children to explore freely without risk of injury.

A child's joy will be even greater if we give him some play dough. It is especially suitable for a young child, because it is relatively easy to clean, and comes in various colors. If that is not available, a modeling clay is also a good option, as is the leftover dough he gets from his mother when she kneads bread. These materials are more than suitable and are dear to the child because he can change their shape. Playing with them develops his sense of spatial forms and stimulates his imagination. Often, as soon as he solves one task, he sets himself another, thereby developing his creativity and problem solving skills. At the same time, his sense of beauty also grows, as he strives to improve his creations. If the teacher discreetly draws the child's attention to some incompleteness, he accepts the feedback and tries to improve his work.

Sand allows even greater freedom in work than most other means, especially when water is available. A child becomes a baker and makes his own bread, an engineer building tunnels, or an artist who conjures up places he has already visited. One can see on his little face that he is deeply involved: He speaks aloud about his plans while his hands are constantly in motion. He creates, enjoys his creation, and celebrates his success.

Children often and spontaneously act out fairy tales they like. Their imagination compensates for the scenery, props, and everything else that creates the illusion of reality in a theater. The value of such play is that the little actors have to imagine how everything will come together—that is, they need to determine their roles and assign functions to various objects using imagination to bring the story to life.

Children frequently change games. They need change, because play helps them to maintain inner balance. If the child was formerly engrossed in a game that required him to concentrate all his thinking and attention, he will afterwards often seek a contrasting activity that allows him to run, jump, and be in motion as much as possible. The length of the game will be determined by his interest in it. The choice of the game should also be guided by the child's inclinations. These interests shift during early childhood, as they are closely tied to the development of the child's instincts. That is why some games naturally disappear from a child's life, while new ones take their place."

Another reason why the choice of games should be left to children is that adult interference reduces the child's ability to explore and discover his own preferences in play, thereby hindering self-discovery. The teacher's constant interference in play has a negative effect by fostering dependence and encouraging passivity. Instead, the teacher's role should be primarily to initiate the game at an appropriate moment, then step back, and allow the child's spontaneity to take over.

Spontaneity is a defining feature of play. Both the choice of activity and its duration should arise naturally, and the play itself should be carried out independently. In short, the primary role of the educator at this stage of life is to provide a supportive environment and appropriate materials that enable the child to develop his mental and physical capacities through self-directed activity.

CHILD'S DRAWINGS

A two-year-old child will already eagerly grab a pencil or a chalk with the greatest joy, if he is given the opportunity to do so, and will test his skills on almost any surface. Like any other form of play, drawing serves to satisfy his desire to engage with the world, which is why he loves it. Just as he expresses his aspirations, longings, and desires through his illusionistic games and storytelling, he conveys his interest in objects, faces, or events through drawing. In this activity, we can find some similarities to artistic creation. However, while both an artist and a child share this longing for expression, they relate differently to both the creative process and its outcomes.

A young child draws primarily for the sake of drawing; he is satisfied with the result, while the artist tends to express inner experiences as precisely as possible and has a critical attitude toward his work.

This aspect of children's creativity has been well studied, largely because children's drawings are easy to collect and preserve. Children love to draw, so there is plenty of material that remains as a visible trace of a young being's passage through different developmental phases, while many other creations deteriorate, get forgotten, or disappear.

For psychologists, children's drawings are of great value as they provide insight into a child's psychological readiness, individuality, and the universal tendencies observed in children across cultures during the first ten years of life. To analyze this, researchers often examine drawings by the same child at different ages to track his developmental progress over time, or compare the drawings of different children of the same age to identify their common and unique traits.

There are also fascinating parallels between children's drawings, the artwork of ancient cultures, and that of so-called primitive peoples. While these share certain common features, a detailed exploration of them is beyond the scope of this work.

The impressions a young child encounters are countless. Before discussing the characteristics of children's drawings, we must first examine their relationship with the world around them. Children begin to notice shapes at an early age. This is evident in the fact that, by the beginning of their second year, they can often recognize images of familiar objects in their environment.

Children also begin to recognize colors early on. Even a two-year-old is not indifferent to his clothing. He likes some clothes more than others. Kornilov cites the example of a little boy who, from the age of two, especially liked purple and dark blue colors—he would stroke them, kiss them, press them against his cheeks. In moments of special tenderness toward his mother, he would call her "my purple one, my bluish one."[1]

By the age of 5, some children already begin to notice the beauty of colors in nature and take pleasure in their harmony. The emergence of this sensitivity depends primarily on the child's individuality, but it is also strongly influenced by the environment in which the child is raised.

> In the example of little Lora E. (4 years, 1 month), given by Stern, one can observe an extraordinary sensitivity to the harmony of colors in nature. She said: "Mother, I want to whisper something in your ear. Yesterday, I felt something so holy in my soul, so very beautiful and sunny. I was in the ice-box room when the sound of bells came in, and then I looked out the window."

Two months later, the same girl said to her mother: "Look here, look how the moon looks holy." Her mother replied: "Why holy?"

> "Because it looks so yellow and beautiful and so evening-like."
> (At the time, the word 'holy' was obviously reserved for something she admired very much because it touched her deeply.)

A child reacts to impressions with his whole personality. He often perceives human qualities in objects and interacts with them on that basis. Sometimes, his response depends on the object's size and the context in which the child encounters it. The child may even alter his voice or the facial expression accordingly.

Let me illustrate this with an example. As I write, the voice of a four-year-old boy playing with dogs drifts through the open window. When he speaks to the smaller dog, his voice becomes thinner, the tone softer than when he addresses the larger one.

A child responds in a similar way to the symbol of an object—for instance, to a drawing that represents it. Stern's son Günter (3 years, 5 months) once drew a pattern and called it a 'scolding hand.' Later, when asked what kind of hand it was, he explained, "It was always forbidding something." In him, this pattern—which bore a vague resemblance to a hand with a raised index finger—immediately evoked the same feelings that real-life situations of that kind used to stir in him.

This tendency to perceive an object as part of a larger situation—and to project onto it the feelings it evokes in us—is not limited to childhood. Even in adulthood, it can occur in certain situations, such as when playing with a small child. By projecting subjective feelings onto objects—seeing more than is actually there and experiencing them through an emotional lens—children

---

1 Konstantin N. Kornilov: *Psihologija Deteta*, p.147. Translated from Russian into Serbian by M. Cvetković.

transfer their perceptions onto symbols, drawings, and pictures. This is why, at first, a child may clearly see something in a drawing that an adult cannot. For example, Groos's little girl, after drawing a single letter, said: "Just look at how sweetly it turns its head." She didn't merely see it as a letter; she perceived its movement and the feeling it evoked in her. For her, it was not just a sign—written beautifully or poorly, as an adult might see it—but a form that had a life of its own.

Although we have identified drawing as one of the most expressive means a child uses alongside speech, the origin of this skill does not lie in the striving for expression, but simply in the child's motor liveliness. The child draws in order to produce movement, and chooses that movement based on imitation. He observes how his parents write and how older children draw and wants to imitate them. Therefore, the age at which a child begins to draw depends on the environment in which he grows up. Some children already start to draw lines as early as their second year of life, often calling them 'writing' rather than drawing, while others may not begin until the age of four. At first, the child simply notices that the movement of his hand produces certain patterns, delights in this discovery, and wants to continue. At this stage he does not yet associate these marks with anything that would remind him of a specific object—he draws purely for the sake of drawing.

This is the stage of **senseless scribbling**, in which the child still draws large longitudinal lines by moving the whole hand. The next step of development proceeds toward small circular and spiral lines, made with a clenched fist. This early scribbling can be compared to cooing, which precedes speech; just as a child's cooing and baby talk prepare him for speaking, so too does doodling serve as a prelude to drawing.

In this process of drawing up, down, here, and there, the child's innate sense for rhythm also comes into play. By repeating the same movements, the child creates almost identical shapes or arranges them into symmetrical patterns, when the motions are reversed. This is how ornamental scribbles emerge. A true sense of ornamentation develops later and is typical of children older than those discussed here.

When an object with decorative elements is placed in front of the children of different ages, their drawings will vary significantly. A five-year-old will typically draw the object without paying any attention to the decoration. About half of eight-year-olds will add the ornamentation, while by the age of sixteen, all children will employ it. For a young child, decoration has no meaning yet—objects are important only insofar as they appear useful to him.[1] Of course, this

---

1 Konstantin N. Kornilov, *Psihologija Deteta*, p.107.

pertains to average children while a more gifted child will notice decorative elements sooner and incorporate them into his drawings.

The child does not remain at he level of scribbling for long. Soon, his drawings begin to bear a distant resemblance to objects, and he names the finished product saying that he drew that specific object. This marks the stage of **scribbling with meaning**. From here, the child progresses to deciding in advance what he will draw. Only at this point can drawing truly be considered a means of expression. Real drawing typically begins around the fourth year of life.

Children's drawings possess a distinctive character. They are not realistic images of objects but instead capture certain significant features—those that hold meaning for the child or capture his attention. For example, when drawing his father, a child may simply draw a circle for the head, add two dots for the eyes, and draw two lines from the head to represent the rest of the body. Similarly, when drawing his mother or another person, the child may use the same shapes. His drawings are symbolic—they function as representations rather than accurate depictions of specific individuals. According to Marie Kerschensteiner, this is called the **schematic stage**. At this stage, the child is not aware of any difficulties in his presentation. He approaches every task, whether self-initiated or assigned, without perceiving it as a challenge.

A 6-year-old child will effortlessly and without hesitation draw a kolo (children in a circular dance) in motion, complete with the music player. He may even indicate that the music player must be paid for his work, by drawing a few small circles in the middle of the ground to represent coins. The distant resemblance of his drawing to what he actually intends to depict, satisfies the child completely, because he is not drawing a specific kolo but rather the general idea of kolo.

Here we encounter the same characteristic observed earlier in discussions of children's imaginative games and inventions—what we previously referred to as a lack of concern for the real appearance of objects. In his drawings, the child does not express everything he knows about an object. He knows that a man has a nose and a mouth, but he often neglects to draw these details. Instead, he draws what is most relevant to him at the moment—what he is thinking as he draws and what the subject represents to him in his inner world.

It is also characteristic that when a child draws a man's head, he will not omit the eyes, and when drawing a house, he almost always includes a chimney with thick smoke billowing from it. The eyes move. The smoke flows from the chimney. The child pays particular attention to elements in motion and seeks to express this motion in his drawing. His people and animals are never at rest—they are moving, doing something, always engaged in some form of activity. This dynamic quality in children's drawing is rightly emphasized by Kornilov: "The tendency of children to endow their drawings with dynamic, even dramatic character, is one of the most important features of children's creativity."

Although, as we have seen, drawing with a predetermined goal occurs early on, it often happens that a child draws one thing and while still working on it moves on to another. I will use the following example to illustrate this fickleness of a small child.

Günter, Stern's son (4 years old at the time), wanted to draw a camel at his parents' request. He began drawing (Fig. 2a), but immediately forgot about the camel because a part of his sketch reminded him of a butterfly's wing. He asked if he should draw a butterfly, erased the upper and lower parts of the first picture, and drew another wing (Fig. 2b). Then he drew another butterfly (Fig. 2c).

> "And now I want to draw a bird—everything that can fly: butterflies, a bird, and then a mosquito." The bird became Fig. 2d.
> "Now a mosquito! Mosquitoes have something to sting with," he said, pressing hard with the tip of the pencil to make two points (Fig. 2e). Suddenly, he was reminded of the moon.
> "Oh, the face of moon. Or should I make the face of sun?" He drew Fig. 2f. Then he went back to the mosquito, drew two points and a curve around them.
> "It's a mosquito." (Fig. 2g). Then he remembered to draw the picture of a bird that was on the wall of the room and started with the beak (Fig.2h). That immediately reminded him of a star, so he said:
> "Let me draw a star" and then made Fig. 2i.

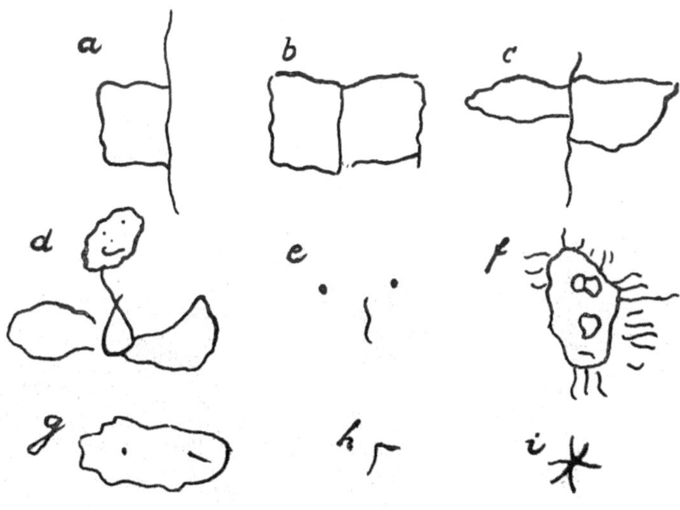

Fig. 2 a–i

These drawings follow a pattern characteristic of childhood imagination: The flow of ideas meanders and the story changes direction with ease. The child's wavering attention flits from one subject to another. The initial intention is often forgotten, because some accidental similarity awakens notions that were not originally considered.The child's synthetic ability is still short-lived.

Often, the child does not depict the correct proportions required by the nature of the object or situation. Instead, a single part may stand out by being of a disproportionate size in relation to the whole. This may be due to his clumsiness and the failure to consider real relationships, or it may represent the child's intention to highlight the most important aspects of the object as he perceives them. H. Werner[1] explains this by stating that feelings play a role in children's creations. He claims that the common trait of children's and primitive peoples' drawings is that the feature that matters the most to the artist is drawn large, while what is not emotionally significant is either omitted altogether or only faintly suggested.

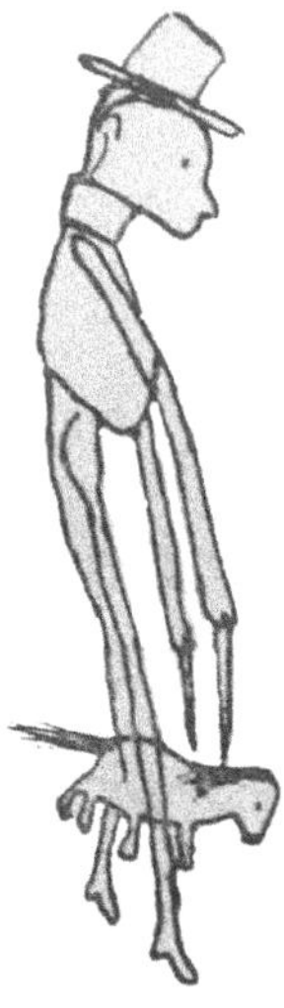

Fig. 3

The drawing in Fig. 3 by a six-year-old girl, clearly illustrates this subjective valuation of objects and their significance. She depicts her father riding a horse, but the horse appears minuscule in comparison. Kunzfeld[2] observes: "Who wouldn't think of certain murals of the ancient Egyptians, in which the pharaoh also towers gigantically over animals and humans?"

---

1 Heinz Werner: *Einführung in die Entwicklungspsychologie*, 1933, p.122.

2 Alois Kunzfeld: *Naturgemässer Zeichen und Kunstfunferricht I*, 1912, p. 46, picture 52.

70

Over time, much like in other activities, the child exhibits increasing synthetic ability. Once he decides on a theme, he executes it with greater attention to the connection between the parts. Around the age of six or seven, a child's drawings begin to resemble reality more closely. Since he is not yet aware of perspective, he draws objects as flat surfaces. This marks the end of the purely schematic stage, as the child now tries to capture the object more accurately.

Before examining the subjects a child draws and his approach to drawing, it is worth noting another characteristic of children's artwork—one frequently seen in younger children and quite unusual from an adult's perspective. A child looking at a picture does not always pay attention to whether it is the right-side up or upside down. Regardless of orientation, he recognizes the essential features of that object and is able to identify it. We encounter this feature in both the children's drawings and in the early attempts at writing. The degree and direction in which a child tilts his work can vary. The examples provided below by Stern effectively illustrate this phenomenon.

The numbers in the far left column of Fig. 4 were written from memory by Stern's daughter Hilda (4 years, 9 months). The rest of the drawing, including the numbers on the right and the head are the product of his daughter Eva (3 years). The children at that age cannot distinguish yet the direction in which the letters appear on a page, nor do they orient them in regard to the objects they represent.

As adults, we occasionally come across a word printed in reverse within a text. In such cases, we are likely to turn the book or newspaper around to read it, as this requires less effort than deciphering it as-is. We do this instinctively because we fully understand that words—like other objects—follow certain directional conventions. A small child has not yet developed this awareness and does not need it. His ability to deviate freely from the standard way of placing the objects on the page—whether to the right, left, up, or down—allows him greater freedom of orientation.

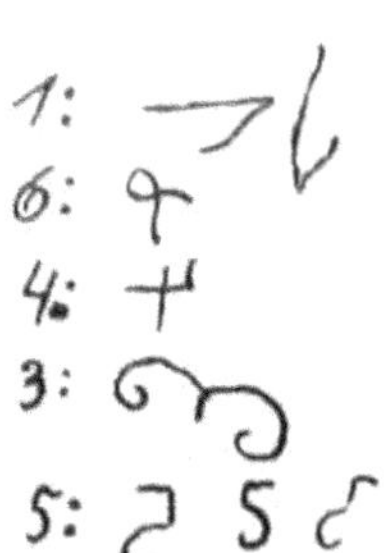

Fig. 4

Regardless of how successful or flawed a child's drawing may be at the age we are examining, it is always drawn from memory. This remains a characteristic of children's drawing for the first eight or nine years of life. A child draws frequently, and sometimes his drawings are even successful from an adult point of view, but the object always remains drawn from memory rather than through direct observation.

Throughout early elementary school, when children draw spontaneously, not all do so with equal skill or with the same sense of meaning. Different children create different schemas, varying in how they enumerate the parts, how they draw them, and how they connect lines to form the whole. In addition to individual variations, there are also differences in schematic development. Over time, these schemas evolve, gradually becoming more representational as children attempt to depict objects more accurately, reflecting how they actually appear.

If a child remains in an early stage of schematic drawing without progressing, it may indicate slow cognitive development or even a developmental retardation. In general, such children tend to draw less frequently than their more gifted peers.

By analyzing how a child draws—whether his lines are broken or smooth, and how he connects the parts into a whole—we can gain valuable insight into his individuality. Therefore, when evaluating a child, we should also consider observations gained from other areas of his work, or at least from a variety of his drawings.

Interestingly, children begin their drawing ventures by representing a person, often paying particular attention to the head. They choose this subject because it is closest and dearest to them. According to their age and development, they will realize their goals by gradually adding more details. Even during the stage of drawing with meaning, the shapes they create often represent human beings.

The two drawings in Fig. 5 made by a four-year-old girl were named after her family members only after she already drew them. The patterns differ from each other; one bears some resemblance to the shape a of person, while in the other, an adult eye would not be able to see anything that would even remotely remind him of a human figure.

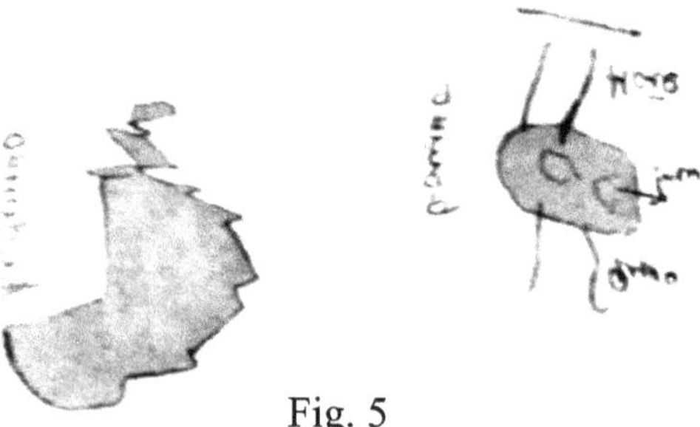

Fig. 5

Later, when child fully enters the schematic stage, his focus shifts primarily to drawing people. These early human figures—often referred to as "cephalopods"—typically feature a round or oval (and very rarely square) head resting directly on legs, often without feet. Sometimes these thin legs end in birdlike toes or include small appendages to suggest feet. Most often, all parts of the head are included. However, a child may become so focused on a particular detail—such as the eyes—that he forgets to draw the nose, mouth, or ears, or just leaves out the nose. In some sketches, all the facial features are present, but the head itself is not outlined, making it appear as though the eyes, nose, and other features are floating in empty space.

It is interesting to note that when a child depicts a person, he often omits the trunk or neck for a long time, but the legs and even the arms are often represented in motion. It is difficult for the child to determine the correct position of the hands in relation to the other parts of the body. As a result, arms may emerge from the head, sprout from the hips, or cross the middle of the body and stretch upward. Even when placed correctly, they often resemble rods, as most of the time do the legs.

Fig. 6 a-e was drawn by a boy (6 years, 6 months). When asked what he had drawn, he himself expressed the difficulty, answering: "A child—only I don't know how to draw hands."

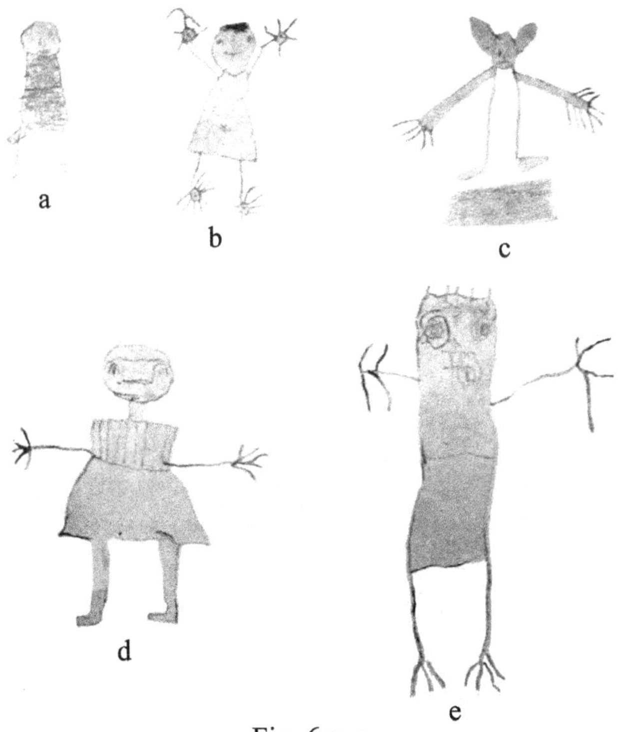

Fig. 6 a–e

The drawing is particularly significant because it comes from a boy who, while looking at illustrations of the fairy tale *The Wolf and the Seven Little Kids*, recalled having seen "a man in the city with three horns on his head." When I asked if he could draw this man, he created the Fig. 6e counting the fingers on his friend's hand as he drew, and then placed five horns on the head. He had most likely seen an intriguing mask during the carnival festivities. The Figs. 6b, 6d, and 6c represent 2 children and a kid, respectively.

As a child progresses from drawing faces to drawing profiles, he often mixes both perspectives for a long time. Thus, in the same picture, the nose may appear both in the middle of the face and on the side. The head is often drawn in profile, while the body is shown from the front, making these drawings reminiscent of ancient Egyptian art.

The two drawings in Fig. 7, catalogued as drawings 35 and 44, were obtained from the Kunzfeld collection.They illustrate beautifully how little the child is concerned with aligning the image with what he intends to represent. He is unaware of the drawing's shortcomings because he has not yet developed a critical view of his own work. For him, the drawing has achieved its purpose and he is satisfied with that.

Fig. 7

Apart from people, animals also occupy an important place in children's drawings, with special attention being paid to domestic animals. They are included wherever possible in the children's games and are treated as beloved companions. It is evident from drawings that children notice and try to express the shapes and the characteristics of specific animal species. Children are especially fascinated by horses. Horses run fast, leap, and thrust their legs forward as they race—no wonder children admire and watch them closely. Children also develop their own schemas for animals, which, as they evolve, increasingly capture the distinctive forms of each species.

74

When a child first attempts to draw an animal, he typically starts with a head which almost always resembles a human head, a round body in a horizontal position, and a number of legs that may not necessarily correspond to the actual animal. It is not uncommon for a horse to have two or three legs, and for a duck to be given four. Usually, the head is drawn from the front, the torso from the side, and all the legs are visible. Sometimes, there is no transition between the head and the trunk. If the animal has horns or another distinguishing feature, it is often included early in the drawing process.

Fig. 8b (a lamb) corresponds completely to this description. Fig. 8a, although it does not follow the same pattern, is still perceived by the child as a horse. In Fig. 8c, which resembles a hippopotamus with its clumsy body and square eyes, we can already see signs of increased skill. All three drawings were made by children between the ages of 4 and 7, but the differences between them are clearly noticeable.

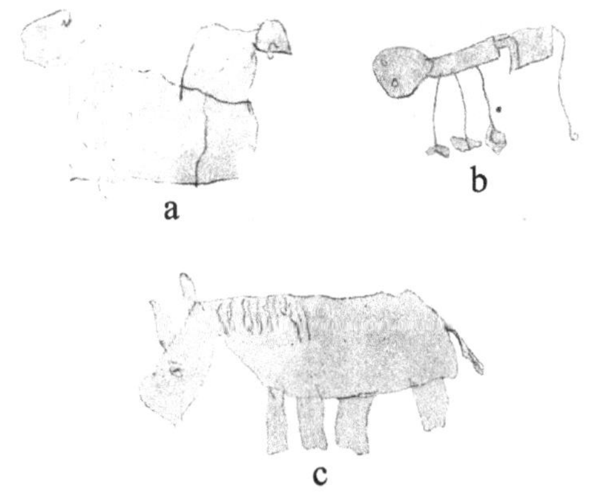

Fig. 8 a–c

The difference in the skill of the two little artists is quite evident in the Figs. 9 a-b, both representing a dog.

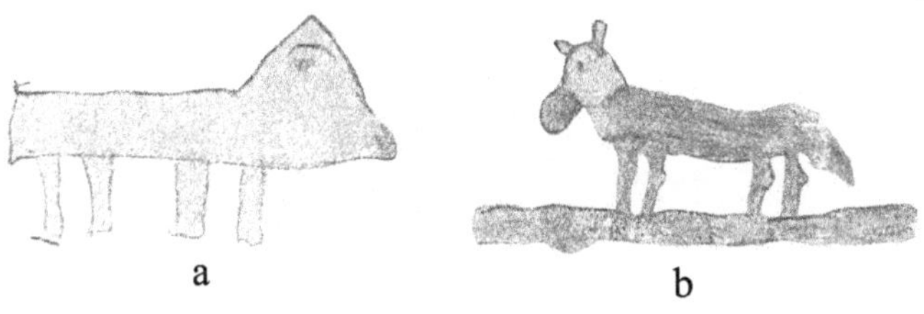

Fig. 9 a–b

Drawings in which the child connects humans with animals are particularly interesting. These scenes depict action, which is precisely why the child enjoys them and likes to draw them. A favorite subject is the horse and the

75

rider. The horse doesn't necessarily have to have four legs, but no matter how many of them there are, all are visible.The rider trying to mount the horse sometimes ends up by standing on it, other times he appears to be passing through it with feet almost touching the ground. He does, however, occasionally manage to sit on the horse properly.

In Fig.10a, for instance, we see a horse with an elongated body and a head resembling a human's, carrying its rider. True, the rider is not seated: he seems to be standing on the horse's body. The young artist is already a keen observer though, because he depicts the rider's face in profile.

The same child depicts a man and a dog in Fig. 10b. This time, a rather broad built man with short legs appears to be standing on his dog, or at best, riding astride. The dog has an unusually long body and a head that resembles a duck.

a   b

Fig. 10 a–b

A child often depicts animals in the company of other animals. In Fig. 11. we see a couple of most unusual combinations. In Fig. 11a, a chicken with very long legs and a thin body stands on a horse whose trunk extends straight from its head and whose legs are as thick as pillars. The chicken stands on tiptoes, as if ready to take off any minute.

a   b

Fig. 11 a–b

76

Even more creativity and composition are evident in Fig. 11b: A mouse and a dog have chosen a table for a pleasant conversation, but a significantly larger cat is attempting to interrupt them. Given its size, the cat will almost certainly catch them.

Compared to animals, plants play a much smaller role in children's spontaneous drawings. This is likely because animals move, allowing children to interact with them, feed them, and observe their behavior—whereas plants remain stationary and less engaging from the child's perspective. When a child chooses to draw plants, he usually depicts trees, often including visible roots. The tree's crown is typically drawn with several curved lines, though sometimes branches appear with fruit placed directly next to the leaves.

Fig 12a shows a simple diagram of a tree. Fig. 12b represents a rose. It gives the impression of a stylized flower similar to those found in traditional handicrafts. In Fig.12c, the little artist captures a peaceful, idyllic scene: next to a flower-filled meadow sit a dog and a cat. Above them, a dove soars through the sky, while the sun—its two eyes watching the scene—seems to gaze down with pleasure.

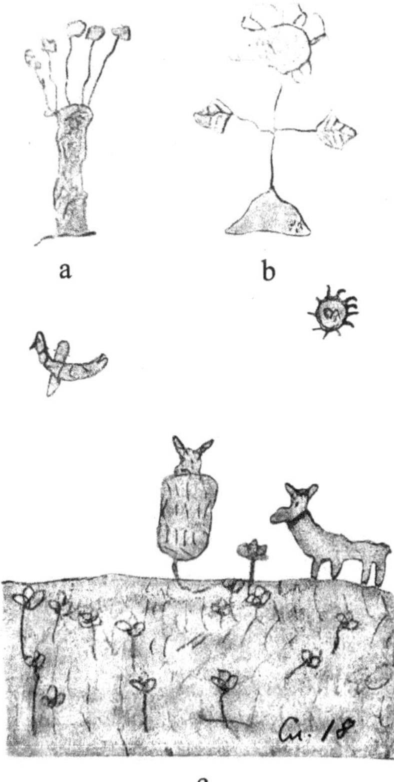

a   b

c

Fig. 12 a–c

Houses, various means of transportation, and utilitarian objects are also frequent subjects of children's drawings, although they appear less often than people and animals. Carts, cars, locomotives, and boats capture their interest, as they are in motion and thus represent life and energy. Houses and other everyday objects relate closely to human activity, which is why children often include them in their drawings. Here, the young artist again focuses on details he is familiar with and the ones that are characteristic for that particular object. Houses are usually drawn from the front, though sometimes three sides are visible. Windows and doors are added regardless of their size or placement—they may be too big, too small, or too high. The chimney, however, will inevitably be there. Everything that is in the house, or rather, everything that the child deems necessary to display—including both things and people engaged in daily activities—can be seen as if the walls were made of glass.

In Fig. 13, the young artist (a boy, 6 years, 6 months) appears to have aimed to depict an airplane performing acrobatic maneuvers in the air. This is no longer just a simple sketch; there is clear skill in the execution of the drawing. The house from which the airplane takes off is only loosely outlined, as it plays a secondary role here, but the thick smoke billowing out of the chimney is still included. The drawing shows that the child is aware of the parts of the airplane.

Fig. 13

The picture of a carriage (Fig.14), despite its shortcomings, conveys a sense of life and movement. The coachman sits with dignity on his seat. The heads of the passengers can be seen through the windows. They must be enjoying the ride, because the horses are in full stride.

We have outlined the main features of objects and characteristics in children's drawings in broad terms. The drawings shown in Figs. 5, 6, and 8-13 were

Fig. 14

created by children in the nursery school in Aleksinac. The sources of other drawings were documented as described.

All preschool children enjoy drawing. Although, these drawings may appear flawed from an adult's perspective, we must acknowledge that they possess a unique charm. The carefree spirit of childhood and the lightness of play hover over them.

When a child draws, his small hand typically moves quickly and confidently across the paper. Drawing in this spontaneous way—without concern for realistic representation—he expresses what interests him or what he knows about an event or object, with affection and without hesitation.

As children develop, their ability to project into the image what is not actually there begins to decline. They become aware that what they intended to express is not fully conveyed, and this realization often leads them to abandon what was once a beloved activity of early childhood. This typically happens at the age of about 8 to 9—the same age, as K. Bühler observes, when children begin to drift away from fairy tales. Letting go of these activities signals that the child has transitioned from the first to the second stage of childhood, leaving behind what no longer feels as appropriate or natural.

It is interesting how something that evokes feelings of admiration and affection in adults—such as a child's naïve chatter, inventiveness, and drawings—has its own special characteristics in early childhood. There is so much spontaneity and liveliness in it all that the young child almost resembles a creative artist. For many children, this phenomenon is temporary. It is almost as if a gift from a benevolent spirit hovered over them. As the child grows stronger, the good spirit retreats. At this stage of development, the spontaneous drawing activity begins to decline. Those who wish to progress further almost always need teaching and guidance.

The exceptions are gifted children, who often travel a considerable part of this path on their own. Some of them, without fully realizing the level of their own artistic ability, draw from memory like other young children do, but their drawings are faithful, finely detailed, and marked by extraordinary liveliness. The child's environment plays a significant role in this, but naturally, both innate talent and personal interest contribute the most.

Even a child around the age of six or seven can sometimes achieve remarkable results. He may create a picture of such expressive power that its origin can only be understood as stemming from the vividness of their mental imagery. It is as if the child looks inward and transfers what he sees in his mind directly onto the paper.

It is not clear whether **eidetic ability** plays a role in this, as it is difficult to determine. However, observations suggest that spontaneous drawing—both in children and in primitive cultures—can appear in two distinct forms: in the form of a schema and in the form of a drawing that depicts the object realistically and with much expression. The following two examples will illustrate these different approaches to children's drawing.

The drawing in Fig. 15 was made by the son of an architect. For years, he drew with passion, focusing especially on fantastical subjects—colorful costumes, fire and hell, and images of the sea (despite never having seen it). His sketchbooks are filled with processions of such drawings.[1]

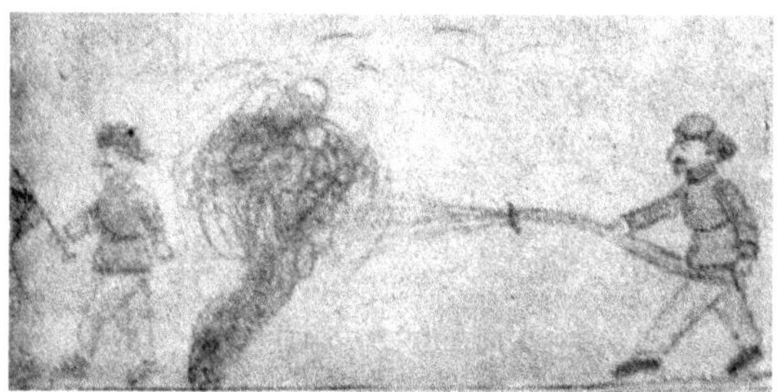

Fig. 15

The drawing in Fig. 16 was created by a five-year-old girl. It points even more to the unusual gift of this child.[2]

If we compare the drawings examined earlier with the last two, we notice a striking difference in skill. However, an unusually strong ability in early childhood is not always necessarily retained. In some cases, it is a fleeting phenomenon that fades as the child grows. Sometimes success in drawing is not general but specific. It is well known that some children especially enjoy

---

1 Reproduced in the work of William Stern: *Psychologie der Frühen Kindheit*, 1930, Tafelanhange, Tafel II.

2 Alois Kunzfeld, *Naturgem. Zeichen u. Kunstunterricht 1*, 1912, p. 55.

Fig. 16

drawing people, while others prefer drawing horses, locomotives, ships, and so on. These special interests vary in duration among different children. Some last only briefly, while others persist. Occasionally, a child carries these interests into the school years.

Naturally, a child with access to the right materials will have more opportunities to nurture his love for drawing than the one without. Therefore it is important to provide these resources whenever possible. Young artists are not particular about materials—old paper bags and scraps of wrapping paper can serve them perfectly well. A sturdy pencil, with a tip that doesn't break easily, allows them to draw without interruption.

Watercolors also bring great joy to the little ones and give them the opportunity to express their creative aspirations to their heart's content. Children love water colors and are happy when they can work with them. By the age of five, they often begin to show a natural feeling for color matching. But even if they don't, it hardly matters. What is most important is that, through drawing, children engage in an activity they genuinely enjoy while developing essential skills: Their hand learns movement, their eye learns to observe, and their imagination learns to create.

Furthermore, if we teach the child to clean up after himself—putting away the paints, washing the brushes, and storing the paper when he is finished—we help cultivate a sense of neatness and cleanliness, as well as foster independence, and enhance the educational value of his efforts.

In addition to these external factors, there is an equally important internal one: the way adults respond to the child and his drawing ability. As long as educators limit their input to providing the necessary materials, the child will draw freely and in connection with his own experiences. If an educator gets involved in what and how the child is creating his art, that involvement must be guided by a deep understanding of the young artist's personality and his unique mode of expression.

We must not judge children's work by adult standards or expect them to depict objects the way we think they should appear. A critical comment or even an ironic smile can destroy a child's enthusiasm for drawing. While children need support and encouragement from adults, that support must respect their individuality and creative freedom. Understanding the nature and characteristics of children's drawings helps teachers avoid harmful judgements. Such missteps can lead a child to abandon his carefree creativity and instead experience bitter feelings, as well as a sense of inadequacy and incompetence. Such feelings not only discourage a young soul, but may also hinder the child's ability to develop their artistic potential.

It is both a shame and a disservice to hinder individual's full development through misguided handling, even when the necessary material conditions are in place. At this stage of life, our interference in the child's creating activity should be minimal. It should consist of tactful and gentle guidance—encouraging the child to look more closely at his work, observe the subject carefully, and perhaps draw it again. This approach almost always increases the child's drawing ability: The second attempt often shows noticeable improvement following such a conversation.

When our influence on the child is indirect rather than direct, his drawings can reveal a great deal—pointing us to important aspects of his individuality and development. If a child stops drawing for an extended period, it should alert the educator to pay closer attention, investigate the root of the problem, and provide support while the child is in their care. However, It is not always necessary to generalize. Sometimes a pause in drawing may have a different cause. Children's development does not follow a strictly linear path; it progresses in cycles. A temporary standstill is to be expected. For teachers, collecting and reviewing children's drawings is an invaluable tool, as it allows them to track and understand each child's development over time.

The task of an educator who aims to foster children's creative abilities is, in short, to provide a harmonious and cheerful environment that allows them to act in a way that suits their nature.

In connection with children's drawing, something should also be said about observing pictures. The sense for both observing and creating appears early and almost simultaneously if the child's living conditions are favorable. Children love to draw because they are creating something on their own. But where does the child's love for pictures come from when he is merely an observer? It comes from the similar strivings we have observed in children at play. Viewing pictures brings diversity and change into a child's life, stimulates his imagination and understanding, and exposes him to beautiful shapes and vivid colors, and thus awakens the feelings of joy.That is why children love a picture. In addition, observing pictures has another influence on the child: It trains him to notice shapes, colors, and sizes, and develops his sense of beauty.

Therefore, children should be given opportunities to view pictures of artistic value, provided they align with the child's level of understanding and interests. The most suitable medium for this is children's picture-books.

Here, too, the children's inclinations should be given priority. For a child to truly benefit from observing pictures, the teacher's guidance is essential. The teacher should encourage close attention to both form and content. When done in a way that feels natural and engaging, this experience can enhance the child's aesthetic sensibility and support overall mental development.

✳✳✳

A child's imagination is a vital part of his creative work. His creations are small, lovely, and filled with liveliness and carefree spirit of childhood. His imagination is spontaneous because it springs from his inner world. All educational activity must be grounded in the child's nature. An educator must approach him with love and a deep understanding of his world in order to provide a supportive environment in which he can grow and develop, guided by his internal drive.

FAIRY TALE AND A CHILD

In 1936, when a discussion about fairy tales appeared in the magazine *Teacher* (*Učitelj*), I decided to contribute as well. I took a different approach than the opponents of fairy tales. Rather than to engage in a theoretical debate, I turned to those most directly concerned: the children themselves. I conducted the surveys in two different ways:

A written survey on the topic of fairy tales conducted among a small number of my fourth-year students (17- to 18-year-olds) at the School of Pedagogy (see Notes).

An oral survey conducted in the classroom with children from first to fourth grade (ages 6 to 10).

The oral survey was carried out twice. The first time with 24 children, and the second with 25. While the initial round of questions focused on the early memories of now nearly grown-up students, the second survey gathered responses from very young children about their immediate surroundings and current experiences. At that time, I did not publish the results of this work.

This year (1940), the *Teacher* is once again addressing the same issue, but the voices now discussing the role of fairy tales are more favorable and sympathetic. Evidently, the perspective on fairy tales—their influence and value—is changing. Perhaps, if I had published my initial investigation earlier, it might have had a greater impact, but I don't believe it will be uninteresting even now (see Notes).

I renewed the experiment this year in a third-grade classroom. It involved 28 children: 24 female and 4 male students.

When evaluating the value of a particular material in the educational process—specifically how much it contributes to the child's development with regard to its purpose—we must, of course, mind both the contents of the material and the characteristics of the child for whom it is intended. A given material may hold one kind of value for the educator who selects it and quite another for the student who receives it. In fact, in some cases, it may have no effect on the student at all. Educational materials will only be beneficial if they are suited to the child who receives them. Just as we would not give an infant food he is not ready to enjoy or digest, we would be equally mistaken to offer intellectual nourishment to a growing child if he is not yet capable of processing it.

We know that children of all strata of society listen to stories from an early age, that they love them and long for them. We should now consider whether fairy tales are merely imposed on children by their environment, or whether this environment, in offering fairy tales to children, has instinctively sensed what they truly need at this stage of life.

This reminds me of Goethe's life. Even during his childhood, there were stormy debates about fairy tales as a great evil. But his mother, an intelligent woman, still told them to him. By the age of seven, he was already inventing fairy tales and sharing them with his friends. And as we know, Goethe became Goethe—not in spite of fairy tales, but perhaps precisely because of them. I say 'because' of them, as they were among the influences that shaped his great creative imagination and, at this tender stage of his life, perhaps even the most important one.

We all know how much children look forward to hearing a good story. There must be something in their soul that craves it, that needs it as surely as the body needs food. To very young children, even their immediate surroundings seem full of the unknown and therefore fascinating. They long to understand it better. How else can this be achieved if not through a story? Their experiences of joy and sorrow are intense. Their emotions are strong and more volatile than those of adults. Can they truly be satisfied by a tale in which the events feel foreign, the thoughts even more incomprehensible, and the situations entirely removed from their own? I think not. There must be something in the tale that resonates with them— something that speaks to their emotions, their understanding, and their capacity to immerse themselves in the story.

When a story is told to a child, he lives in it, rejoices with it, and shares it—creating his own interpretation of it. Everything he hears comes alive. Houses, people, palaces, huts, and forests are not just words to a child; they all evoke vivid images in his mind. The experiences unfold one after another because the fairy tale is all action, all plot. A child's imagination— alive and ever-moving, like the child himself—follows these events, and in doing so, it grows and strengthens. It is because of those images and emotions, and because of his active participation in creating them, that a child loves a fairy tale.

Why wouldn't he be just as pleased to learn about what occurs in the air, water, and so on? Because if you wanted to spark a child's interest in those subjects, you would have to present them in the guise of fantasy. A child is concerned with other children, people, and phenomena related to him. To a child, the lives of children and their concerns are closer to him than the lives and sufferings of adults. The child has no interest in things as such, only in the way they are connected to him.

All of the above statements are, more or less, well known facts. They were confirmed by the results of my survey in which twelve of my students participated.

86

These students were in the fourth grade at a State Pedagogy School, preparing to become teachers. At their age, they still maintained a lively interest in their own childhood and the memories associated with it. Their many early recollections surfaced with surprising clarity, emerging from the depths of memory, becoming clearer at this stage of their development. In other words, the significance of those memories—and their meaning in relation to other life experiences—became clearer to those who had lived them.

When I initiated this survey, I was motivated by the impressions I had retained from my own childhood. The way I now understand these impressions as an adult was confirmed by the survey.

Six of the interviewees recalled that, as children, they did not distinguish fairy tales from reality. Two others sometimes had a vague sense that the stories were not real, but even after their elders confirmed their suspicions, they still enjoyed listening to them.

They also remember being afraid at times, yet they eagerly immersed themselves in the stories.

According to one student: "Despite the fear I felt when listening to such stories, and the recurring dream they caused, I still loved hearing those tales."

All the interviewees reported a particular fondness for stories with fantastic elements. Some even described the vividness with which these characters appeared to them—it was as if they could actually see them. They developed strong emotions toward these imaginary figures.

Naturally, the heroes of those stories are fairies, witches, princes, kings. Already at that age, some have heard about Prince Marko (see Notes) and felt deep sadness over his suffering. These stories evoke various emotions, such as compassion and gratitude (for example, when the prince saves Cinderella), a sense of justice (such as hatred toward the wolf in *Little Red Riding Hood*), and fear.

But the fear of traveling Gypsies was just as intense; one respondent noted that fear can be caused not only by the mysterious heroes of fairy tales, but also by real-life figures who are used to threaten children with harm to their well-being and survival. (They were said to come into town to take away 'bad' children and make them live in a caravan.)

The first fairy tales—*Little Red Riding Hood* and *The Wolf and the Seven Little Kids*—are highly instructive, often more so than parental advice and instructions. When a child hears what happens to Little Red Riding Hood, he knows that she suffered because of her disobedience, making him less likely to stray far from home. Similarly, *The Wolf and the Seven Little Kids* carries a strong moral lesson.

Psychologically speaking, this observation is of great interest. It highlights the nature of preschool children: When it comes to behavior, they are more influenced by lessons conveyed through stories than by direct instructions from adults. A lesson presented in the form of a story is easier for them to grasp than a mere admonition. To a child, a fairy tale is concrete—it vividly illustrates the consequences of disobedience. In contrast, advice and instructions are just pale words, quickly forgotten.

The stories that are too explicitly instructive are also not well liked. A fairy tale affects a child much like a good novel affects adults. It does not have to be tendentious to evoke deep thoughts and feelings; it appeals to our aesthetic and ethical sensibilities. It achieves this by vividly depicting its environment and reaching into the depths of the soul. The fairy tale introduces a child to the lives of beings similar and familiar to him. By portraying these characters' experiences in simple yet powerful imagery, it imparts knowledge and fosters understanding through experience.

One student reported the following: "I only remember the feeling with which I listened to *Cinderella*. Today, no other version of *Cinderella* can awaken the same emotion I felt back then. I connected with the characters—I imagined meeting Cinderella on my way to church and believed that her stepmother lived somewhere behind our house. I thought of the Prince with humility, my eyes filled with gratitude for saving Cinderella. Overwhelmed by feelings— the fear I felt when the stepdaughter secretly went to church, the anxiety of her losing her slipper, and the joy of seeing Cinderella beside the Prince—I was dumbfounded. I didn't know what to say, except to ask to hear it again."

Two interviewees (both female students) also shared their interpretations. They invented completely new creations in connection with some specific persons and events, or adapted the stories they had heard."I just rearrange it the way I think," says one of those students. Some interviewees also expressed their desire to possess the qualities of the fairy tale heroes— beauty, wealth, and happiness.

From the perspective of those who believe education should focus solely on achieving realistic goals, this aspect of a fairy tale could also be seen as a flaw—in life, some desires can never be fulfilled. A child will not become a prince or a princess and may end up being unhappy. But is this really so? The desires that arise in childhood, connected to tangible values as beauty, wealth, and happiness are merely signs of striving for something greater. With development, this striving will evolve and change its goal, but it will remain in the soul as a force that propels one forward. After all, in all of us, young and old alike, that striving for something more beautiful and better never truly stops, even as our concept of "beautiful" and "better" changes in the course of life. Why should this striving be denied to children?

88

Now, let us turn to the second part of the examination. As previously mentioned, in this section I addressed the children directly.

During the first examination I used *Politics for Children* (see Notes). I read two stories to my young listeners: one was a well-known cautionary tale about dwarfs by Milica Janković (see Notes); the other told of adventures and misadventures of a little hen. The first story was fantastical, while the second, about the hen, was closer to the children's own experiences. Yet, more children preferred the story about the dwarfs.

During the second phase of examination, I told the children stories I had invented myself. One was a fairy tale called *Land of Laughter*. Everything in it was cheerful and pleasant—but also impossible. The other story, about poor children, was ordinary and rooted in everyday life. And yet, the majority of children—16 out of 25—found *Land of Laughter* more beautiful.

In both cases, I asked the children which story could have actually taken place. Most of them understood the question perfectly well, yet they were more drawn to fantastic stories. Why? One child responded: "Because everything is beautiful there." The most interesting thing is that the 4th grade students, in particular, fell in love with *Land of Laughter*. They were captivated by its cheerfulness and rich colors, even though they fully understood that its content was unrealistic.

This year, I examined 28 third-grade children: 24 girls and 4 boys. And again, I told two stories. The first one was closer to the children in terms of content, because it talked about the friendship between two girls. The second was about a doll carved from wood by a young shepherd—a doll that came to life but, after various experiences, eventually returned to being an inanimate object. Thus, the content of the second story was fantastical.

Only six girls thought the first story was more beautiful, although they also mentioned liking the second one, as well. The rest preferred the second story.

During this examination, I slightly adjusted my method. To prevent the children from influencing each other when expressing their opinions, I first asked them to write down which story they liked more and why. Since it is well known that third graders still struggle with expressing their thoughts in writing, I followed up with a conversation, which provided deeper insight into their understanding.

They liked the second story more—"it is better, because everything is beautiful in it," although some were not happy with the ending. "Why does the girl become a doll again? That is so sad." From both, the oral and written responses, I have concluded that this story was considered better, because it featured a variety of scenes, some cheerful, some sad, which made it more dynamic and engaging.

The endings of both stories saddened the children. They wished the friends did not separate and that the girl-doll did not return to her original wooden state. Children, it seems, prefer a happy ending.

They all understood that the story about friends could have happened. "There are girls like that, and there are even better ones," said one little girl. Yet, she still found the second story, with the doll, more beautiful, explaining: "everything is beautiful in it." She didn't mind that it was 'just a story' and couldn't have happened in real life.

Of course, if one asks further what exactly makes it beautiful, one will hear a list of details. At times, one may even catch a glimpse of something deeper. But simply observing the children's expressions while listening to the story makes it clear—they are experiencing something enchanting, something that completely captivates them. Even if a child cannot articulate in detail what makes the story so attractive, the fact that they overwhelmingly associate beauty with the second story, despite knowing it is unrealistic, shows that they enjoy it for what it is—for its content and its beauty as such.

One child found the idea of a mouse dragging the doll-girl underground hilarious. Perhaps he imagined the scene more vividly, making it funnier to him. This goes along with the fact that children prefer stories with happy endings—they obviously appreciate the cheerfulness and the joy that the fairy tale offers.

Now, let us analyze the results of the surveys that involved the children directly. In every case discussed above, the children overwhelmingly chose the story with a fantastical content. What does this tell us?

It is clear that a child prefers a story that fuels his imagination, that he loves it even when he knows it is not true. He enjoys it much like we enjoy drama, film, art— these forms of storytelling which offer richness and open up a broader perspective. One might argue that realistic stories do this, as well. Without a doubt, they do, but since they rarely provide the same colorfulness and abundance of events, they have a lesser impact on a child's imagination.

Children love illusions; they love to immerse themselves in beauty—the kind of beauty that is accessible to them and can be enjoyed even when it is obvious that what they are experiencing is not true. By the fourth grade of primary school, children have already outgrown the stage in which they struggle to distinguish reality from fantasy— we know that. So how is it that even those who—now older—read fairy tales less often but still find these stories beautiful?

They do so precisely because they know the story is not real, but they enjoy the action and the fantastic representations of events for their own sake, without connecting them to the reality.

In this latest survey, there surfaced some very interesting details, all pointing to yet another way in which the fairy tales influence the development of young children.

Ten children highlighted the instance of helping a child-doll (adopted in the story by a kind lady). Six of these children were the same ones who preferred the story about friendship over the one with a more fantastical theme. They did so specifically because of its ethical and social values. One little girl who seemed to be guided by just such motives, said: "I like the first story because Ljubica used to visit Radmila when she was sick." Another child said she liked the story because "the lady took the girl with her and cared for her."

One boy, however, expressed a different opinion: He didn't like the story about these two girls because they weren't really good friends. "It was Ljubica's fault. Radmila had to call her to come." It is clear from this case that children, just like adults, have the ability to immerse themselves in the situations of people close to them. Just the fact that ten interviewees emphasized the episode of helping someone in the story is significant enough. It shows that beyond mere entertainment—which provides children with the illusory pleasure of exploring worlds that real life does not offer—fairy tales also affect their emotions and moral development. They ennoble the soul.

This is most clearly confirmed by the statement of one little boy, who grasped the deeper meaning of this fairy tale better than most of his classmates. He liked the story about the doll, saying "Because that teacher sent the shepherd boy to learn how to share, and I also like that the lady took the little girl under her wing. But I don't like that the little girl was naughty, so the dwarf turned her back into a doll." He added he would have liked it even better if the doll-girl had been obedient, so that she wouldn't have had to turn back into a doll.

A fairy tale is primarily nourishment for the soul of a preschool child. It is particularly relevant at this stage because it aligns with the child's mental structure. Even when an older child reads or listens to a fairy tale, he consciously enjoys its vivid imagery and colorfulness.

Some might criticize me for analyzing school-age children, while emphasizing the value of fairy tales for preschool-age children. However, I believe that if a fairy tale, or a memory of one, continues to resonate with a school-age child, who is already more observant and reflective, then its impact on a preschool-age child must be even deeper, stirring even stronger emotions. This idea is supported by the results of a survey conducted among the female students in the fourth grade of the school for teachers mentioned above.

A fairy tale cannot divert the human spirit from the path of development or create fantasists and incompetents, because a child naturally outgrows it as he matures and becomes receptive to other influences—just as he outgrows his toy horses, dolls, teddy bears, and, in general, the games of early childhood. It is merely a tool of this stage of life, just another form of play, like everything else a child experiences and creates during this time.

When we compare the analysis of the adult students' statements with the results of the examination of elementary school children, I find a clear alignment of facts. I believe I can say that, through this small study, I have demonstrated the necessity of fairy tales for children.

Children need fairy tales just as adults, beyond their daily work, need special moments that uplift them, strengthen them, and reveal aspects of their soul that may go unnoticed even by themselves in the monotony of everyday life. However, fairy tales are even more essential for children than these moments are for adults, because they contribute not only to their spiritual growth but also to their overall development, helping them become more complete individuals.

This work is about the fairy tales in general and their significance for early childhood. Naturally, the choice of a fairy tale depends on the teacher's judgement. No one forces us to tell stories that contain frightening elements—we select them and adapt them according to the needs of the child. In this, we have complete freedom.

If we notice that a child does not enjoy a particular fairy tale or that it has a negative effect on him, we should refrain from telling it. A fairy tale is merely a tool, like any other in education. We use it when it has a positive influence and discard it when it does harm, but let us not force a child's soul into our adult molds before it has had the chance to develop naturally.

Let us not insist that a child be practical and grounded in reality at an age when reality is farther from him than a fantastic fairy tale.

<h1 style="text-align:center">TRANSLATOR'S NOTES:</h1>

<h3 style="text-align:center">FOREWORD</h3>

To Quote (page v) and **Review** (page viii) – Prof. Dr. Nada Todorov: "The Interpreting of Fairy Tales by Ruža Lerinc: the Beginnings of Theory of Reception" ("O tumačenju bajki Ruže Lerinc: počeci teorije recepcije"); a review of "Fairy Tale and a Child," published in 2010, in journal *Lamed*.

In the Words (page vii) and **Commemorative** (page viii) – Dragomir Filipović: An article "Remembering Aleksinac in school year 1940/41" ("Sećanje na Aleksinac godine 1940/41"), published as an article in *At the Source of Teaching – 120 Years of the Teacher's School and Pedagogical Academy in Aleksinac* (*Na izvorištu Učiteljstva – 120 godina Učiteljske škole i Pedagoške akademije u Aleksincu*), published in 1991.

Chapter (page viii) – Milan Petrović, Zoran Stevanović and Siniša Golubović: *Aleksinac and Pomoravlje in the past* (*Aleksinac i Pomoravlje u prošlosti*) published 2021. A comprehensive history including a chapter dedicated to Ruža Lerinc (pp. 401-413) with a moving contribution by Dragomir Filipović.

In 2022 (page viii) – The *Ruža Lerinc* prize-winning video project was authored and submitted by Emilija Pešić to the Hannah (an EU youth-competition with a historical subject). It was based on the scientific work "Ruža Lerinc, professor at the State school for teachers in Aleksinac" by Milan Petrović and Zoran Stevanović, the history professors. The video is uploaded on YouTube under the title *Emilija Pešić-"Ruža Lerinc."*

<h3 style="text-align:center">IMAGINATION OF A SMALL CHILD</h3>

His (page 3) – In keeping with the tone and conventions of the original 1937 edition, masculine pronouns ("he," "him," "his") are used throughout when referring to the child. This reflects the societal norms of the period and is not intended to suggest gender exclusivity.

Similarly, to maintain the historical and cultural context of the time, the term "Gypsies" is retained where it appeared in the original text, although the term Roma is preferred today as more respectful and accurate.

Abriss Geistigen (page 6) – The scientific works cited by the author are given in their original language for cross reference purposes. These works remain foundational to modern science and are still generally accessible online. When referring to well-known figures, the author often used last names only. Full names and the original titles are provided in footnotes.

Vrbica (page 45) – A spring holiday celebrated on Lazarus Saturday, commemorating Jesus Christ's resurrection of Lazarus from the dead. It is one of the most revered holidays among Serbs, and also one of the most joyful. On this day, young children parade through towns carrying bells and small garlands made of bent willow branches. The name Vrbica comes from the Serbian word vrba, meaning "willow."

Kolo (page 59) – A traditional circular or semicircular folk dance widely performed in Serbia. The word *kolo* means "circle" or "wheel" in Serbian. Dancers of all ages hold hands and move in fast rhythmic patterns, often accompanied by lively folk music. Kolo is an UNESCO-inscribed, powerful symbol of cultural identity, unity, and community, and remains one of the most beloved group activities, especially among young children.

Prince Marko (Kraljević Marko) (page 87) – A Serbian historical figure who lived in the 14th century and became a legendary symbol of resistance to Ottoman rule. His fame was so great that even small children knew of him through epic poetry.

FAIRY TALE AND A CHILD

School of Pedagogy (page 85, paragraph 2) – In Serbia during the 1930s, only a handful of nursery schools existed, primarily in major urban centers. Other small towns may have had individual nursery schools, but these were usually private, church-affiliated, or charity-based rather than state-run. Nursery schools typically accepted children between the ages of 3 and 7. Their primary goal was to prepare children for formal elementary education by developing basic social, motor, and cognitive skills through play and structured activities. While nursery schools were not directly part of elementary system, they were often affiliated with it, particularly within teacher training programs. Given that the State School of Pedagogy in Aleksinac trained future educators, it is likely that the nursery school founded by Ruža Lerinc was connected to this institution, serving as a practice school for student teachers.

I don't think it will be uninteresting even now (page 85, paragraph 5) – I discovered Ruža Lerinc's article "Fairy Tale and a Child" in 2020, purely by chance, while conducting online research. Originally published in Serbian in 1940, in the monthly magazine *Teacher*, it struck me as a perfect companion piece to the chapter "Fairy Tale" in this book. I have therefore decided to include it here.

Politics for Children (Politika za decu) (page 89) – A children's book written by Bojan Ljubenović, published in 1921. It was designed to introduce young readers to political concepts in simple, engaging, and often humorous way. This unique book was quite ahead of its time.

Milica Janković (page 89) – A contemporary of Ruža Lerinc, Milica Janković was a Serbian writer of prose and verse who often focused on themes of

94

women's rights, education, and social issues. Her writing often depicted the struggles of women in a patriarchal society, exploring topics such as gender inequality, family expectations, and personal growth. A dedicated teacher, she was also known for her contributions to children's literature and educational writing.

Her best-known children's story titled *The Dwarfs* (*Patuljci*), is a charming symbolic tale that dwells on deeper social and moral themes.The story follows a group of mysterious, kind-hearted dwarfs who secretly help people in their village. They work at night, doing good deeds without expecting any reward or recognition. However, when the villagers start to take their help for granted and become greedy, the dwarfs disappear, leaving the people to ponder the value of kindness and selflessness.